BUCYRUS

MAKING THE EARTH MOVE
FOR 125 YEARS

KEITH HADDOCK

MBI

First published in 2005 by MBI, an imprint of
MBI Publishing Company, Galtier Plaza, Suite 200,
380 Jackson Street, St. Paul, MN 55101-3885 USA

The information in this book is true and complete to
the best of our knowledge. All recommendations are
made without any guarantee on the part of the author
or Publisher, who also disclaim any liability incurred
in connection with the use of this data or specific
details. We recognize that some words, model names,
and designations mentioned herein are the property
of the trademark holder. We use them for identification
purposes only.

MBI titles are also available at discounts in bulk quantity
for industrial or sales-promotional use. For details
write to Special Sales Manager at MBI Publishing
Company, Galtier Plaza, Suite 200, 380 Jackson Street,
St. Paul, MN 55101-3885 USA.

ISBN-13: 978-0-7603-2286-4
ISBN-10: 0-7603-2286-4

Editor: Steven Gansen
Designer: Mandy Iverson

Printed in China

About the author:

Keith Haddock is an authority on earthmoving
equipment with a career spanning thirty-five years in
the earthmoving and surface mining industries,
including many years as manager of engineering for
Luscar Ltd. Haddock has been responsible for several
Alberta, Canada, historical preservation projects at the
Diplomat Mine Interpretive Centre and the Reynolds
Alberta Museum. In 1985, he cofounded the Historical
Construction Equipment Association based in Bowling
Green, Ohio. He is a Fellow of the Canadian Institute
of Mining and a registered Professional Engineer in
Alberta, Canada.

Since retiring from Luscar in 1998, Haddock has
been a full-time author and freelance writer on
heavy equipment. His articles have appeared in such
publications as *Construction Equipment*, *Engineering
News Record*, *Canadian Heavy Equipment Guide*, *Tracks
& Treads*, *Earthmovers* (U.K.), *Classic Plant & Machinery*
(U.K.), and *Cranes Today* (U.K.). He has served as a
research consultant for numerous cable television
programs, appearing on the History Channel, the
Discovery Channel, and the Learning Channel. His
other books for MBI include *Giant Earthmovers: An
Illustrated History*, *Colossal Earthmovers*, *Extreme Mining
Machines*, *Classic Caterpillar Crawlers*, *Earthmover
Encyclopedia*, and *Heavy Equipment*.

CONTENTS

FOREWORD

In December 2005 Bucyrus will officially celebrate its 125th year of existence. The significant engineering and manufacturing feats successfully accomplished during its long tenure have solidified Bucyrus' role as a true American icon. From our humble 1880 beginnings as the Bucyrus Foundry and Manufacturing Company in Bucyrus, Ohio, to modern day Bucyrus International, Inc. in South Milwaukee, Wisconsin, we continue to build the world's largest excavators. You will find another common theme as you trace our history—we have remained steadfastly true to our role as the leader in excavator technology and innovation.

The combination of various companies that have comprised our corporate identity over the past 125 years reflects 667 years of excavator design and manufacturing expertise. We have produced over 150,000 machines utilizing more than 1,100 patents. Those patents created some of the first commercially accepted steam shovels; the walking dragline; the first commercially accepted rotary blasthole drill; rope crowd electric mining shovels; the world's largest single-bucket excavator, Big Muskie; the Space Shuttle transporter; and the first excavators to use the highly efficient AC electrics technology, to name only a few.

In this our 125th year of existence, it is interesting to note that we have returned to our roots. Over the years, Bucyrus had diversified into machinery for civil construction, marine cranes (for servicing offshore oil drilling platforms), water well drills, and specialty gear cases for the aerospace and defense industries. Today, we manufacture machines exclusively for surface mining; our very first machines were also built to serve such large-scale excavation projects. At current-day replacement value, we have an installed machinery base of over $10 billion—the largest of any surface mining machinery company in the world.

Looking forward from 2005, Bucyrus faces some unique economic situations. The worldwide commodity markets are surging as the result of unprecedented demand from China. As the Chinese economy of 1.3 billion people enters into full-blown industrialization, demand for commodities, and therefore for our machines that mine these commodities, has reached historic proportions. Although the cycle has only just begun, Bucyrus is experiencing record-breaking financial performance, with equipment and aftermarket backlogs growing at unprecedented rates. Considering the Chinese economy has the potential over time to be four times that of the United States, we believe we are in an economic cycle that will last for many years to come.

Although it is difficult to display all of our various engineering and manufacturing accomplishments over the past 125 years, this book provides a visually rich experience of some of Bucyrus' more unique endeavors, giving readers the opportunity to see the scale and type of machinery that we have provided for various industry applications during our history.

During Bucyrus' first 100 years there were only eight presidents; the tenure of William Coleman alone spanned 32 years. Although I cannot match Bill Coleman's longevity, I am honored to serve as the 14th president of Bucyrus in the 125th year of Bucyrus history.

I hope you enjoy your historical review of our company. In a sense, this book merely marks yet another milestone in our long and illustrious history. We are dedicated to mirroring our past success by creating new success stories as we move into our next 125 years.

Timothy W. Sullivan
President & CEO
Bucyrus International, Inc.

PREFACE

It was an honor to be asked to write this 125th Anniversary book for Bucyrus International, Inc. My association with the company goes back to childhood days in England where the name Ruston-Bucyrus, the British affiliate, conjured up magic for a small boy fascinated by large excavating machines. This early interest in earthmoving evolved into a career in heavy construction and surface mining, and my interest in excavating machines encompassed not only my work but also my hobbies. The companies I worked for were all customers of Bucyrus-Erie, enabling me to become very familiar with its products. I now own a 1941 Bucyrus-Erie model 10-B excavator as a hobby machine.

Few manufacturing companies today can claim 125 years of continuous production. In fact, the site of the main plant and corporate offices has remained in South Milwaukee, Wisconsin, since 1893. During the 1990s, I was involved with the restoration of a Bucyrus dragline built in 1917. The restoration team was amazed that Bucyrus could supply a set of original drawings for this machine and to learn that modern machines are still being built in the same factory as the old-timer was built in some 80 years earlier.

My special thanks go to Kent Henschen, Director–Marketing at Bucyrus, from whom I received full cooperation throughout the preparation of this book. I was also privileged to gain access to Bucyrus' extensive archives of documents and images. It was my pleasure to work with Kent and his enthusiastic production team of Ron Gratzke, Robert Jelinek, Jennifer Okonek, and Denise Peterson. And special thanks go to David Lang, Director of Engineering, Shovels and Drills, whose personal interest in the company's history was invaluable in providing information and verifying all the facts and figures.

I hope you enjoy reading this book about a dynamic company that has changed with the times and continues to change to meet customers' needs. Bucyrus has always been proud of its history, recording milestones and achievements in various publications including *Designed for Digging*, commemorating 75 years in business, and *100 Booming Years*, marking the company's centennial. We look forward to continuing this 25-year cycle with another book to commemorate 150 years of Bucyrus machines in 2030.

INTRODUCTION

Bucyrus International, Inc. boasts an unmatched heritage of specialization in the mining and construction equipment manufacturing industry. From the smallest yard crane to some of the largest machines ever to roam the earth, no other company has produced such a wide variety of types and sizes of excavating machines. Its floating dredges, tractor equipment, cable excavators, hydraulic excavators, drills, cranes, walking draglines, bucket wheel excavators, and other special equipment have made the name Bucyrus synonymous with making the earth move for 125 years.

Over those years, Bucyrus (and also under former corporate names—Bucyrus Foundry and Manufacturing Company, Bucyrus Steam Shovel and Dredge Company, The Bucyrus Company, and Bucyrus-Erie Company) has led the industry in innovative products designed to satisfy the world's toughest earthmoving requirements. Along the way, Bucyrus has bolstered its capabilities and diversified its product lines by strategically acquiring manufacturing rights or purchasing other significant companies, such as the Vulcan Steam Shovel Company, Atlantic Equipment Company, Erie Steam Shovel Company, Monighan Manufacturing Corporation, Armstrong Drill Company, Ransomes & Rapier Ltd., and Marion Power Shovel Company.

Recent acquisitions and rationalization of its product lines have transformed the company from a provider of many products to a multitude of industries into a company specializing in service, support, and manufacturing of surface mining equipment. Today's products—shovels, walking draglines, and drills—benefit from a combined design and manufacturing expertise of more than 600 years.

Throughout its history, Bucyrus' research and development efforts have continued to add new products and improve established product lines with a focus on reducing the cost per ton of material moved. Today, with 125 years of achievements, Bucyrus International, Inc. continues to meet the needs of surface mining customers worldwide with leading technology products, high-quality OEM parts, and dedicated service professionals, ensuring the highest level of machine productivity and dependability.

CHAPTER ONE

CORPORATE HISTORY—
THE BUCYRUS LEGACY

THE EARLY YEARS

In 1880, Daniel P. Eells of Cleveland, Ohio, brought together a group of relatives and prominent business associates with the intention of forming a new company for the manufacture of railroad and mining equipment. The railroads were expanding west, and Eells saw an opportunity to benefit from the expansion and wanted to be on the forefront of the industry. The group Eells created purchased the former Bucyrus Machine Company of Bucyrus, Ohio, and on December 28, 1880, the new company was officially incorporated as Bucyrus Foundry and Manufacturing Company. Its charter was ". . . to carry on the business of a foundry and of manufacturing machinery and railroad cars . . . ."

Mr. Eells was already a well-known name in the Ohio business world, having become president of the Commercial National Bank of Cleveland in 1868. He was subsequently connected with several prominent railroad and coal companies, and by 1895, he was associated in a senior capacity to thirty-two different corporations. He had become very familiar with starting and operating businesses during the turbulent financial period of the late 1800s.

In the spring of 1882, the Bucyrus Foundry and Manufacturing Company received its first steam shovel order from the Ohio Central Railroad. The machine was known as the Thompson Iron Steam Shovel and Derrick,

Opposite: Taken in 1872, this is one of the earliest photographs of a steam shovel in action. This shows an Otis shovel working on the Midland Railroad at Paterson, New Jersey. William S. Otis built the first steam shovel in 1835, but relatively few others were built until Bucyrus introduced the Thompson shovel in 1882.

The steam shovels built by the Bucyrus Foundry and Manufacturing Company earned a solid reputation for reliability in railroad construction. The 70C (chain hoist) was one of the most popular in the early twentieth century. Employed mostly on railroad construction, this type of heavy-duty half-swing machine became known as a railroad shovel.

named after its designer, John Thompson, the manufacturing manager at the company. Shovel sales to the Northern Pacific Railroad and to the Savannah, Florida & Western Railroad shortly followed, and all were delivered within a few months.

The following year, railway equipment from the company was exhibited at the National Exposition of Railway Appliances in Chicago, and Bucyrus' Thompson Shovel won first prize. This early publicity and reports of excellent performance generated further sales, which reached 59 machines sold by 1889.

The company soon expanded into manufacturing other types of excavating machinery and shipped its first dipper dredge in 1883. By 1889, Bucyrus was able to boast in its sales literature, "We have by far the largest and best equipped shops in the country for the manufacture of steam shovels and dredges."

MOVE TO SOUTH MILWAUKEE

In the period between 1889 and 1891, the company's product line was shifting toward larger machines, and Bucyrus management found the production facilities at Bucyrus, Ohio, to be increasingly inadequate. Additional foundry, machining, and erecting facilities were needed, as well as storage space for raw materials, castings, and finished products. The 1.5-acre (0.6-hectare) site in Ohio did not permit expansion of the type required, and there was no prospect of acquiring additional land adjacent to the existing plant.

In the fall of 1891, a group known as the South Milwaukee Company made a presentation to Bucyrus' management. The group was promoting an industrial town on property it held in the Oak Creek Township of Milwaukee County, Wisconsin. The site offered was located about ten miles south of Milwaukee on the shores of Lake Michigan and had been farmed until 1890. The site held great potential, as it was adjacent to the Chicago & North Western Railroad tracks and offered the possibility of access to lakefront docks via a proposed railway. The site not only seemed perfect for the

In 1890, the company changed its corporate name to the Bucyrus Steam Shovel and Dredge Company to reflect the significance of dredges in its business. Many of the dredges were used in gold mining, such as this elevator dredge shipped to the Pomeroy Company of Portland, Oregon, in 1898.

From 1904 to 1908, Bucyrus shipped 77 steam shovels to the Panama Canal construction site, one of the greatest excavation projects of the twentieth century. Most of these shovels were the giant 95-ton model, the largest available at the time. The Panama business brought Bucyrus valuable experience in building successive machines in large lots.

company's present and future needs, but the South Milwaukee Company offered a substantial financial incentive to clinch the deal. Plans were immediately put into action to uproot the established company in Ohio and move it to the new location in South Milwaukee, Wisconsin.

Operations at the South Milwaukee plant commenced in April 1893, with about fifty workers employed. The transition was not completed until later in the year, however, as several large shovels and dredges had to be completed in the old plant before shipment. Most of the workers at the Ohio plant were offered jobs in Wisconsin, and approximately 10 percent ultimately made the permanent move to South Milwaukee. In August 1893, the company was incorporated with the new name of Bucyrus Steam Shovel and Dredge Company of Wisconsin.

The first few years at the new plant in South Milwaukee proved very difficult for the company. The new and relatively unskilled labor force posed problems of training, recruiting, and housing. Production was down

as the shovel and dredge market softened and increased bank borrowings became the order of the day. Eventually, financial difficulties led to reorganization of the company and, in 1896, a name change to The Bucyrus Company. It was during this time that Bucyrus management determined that the special-purpose excavating machines drove the company's future progress and that Bucyrus' resources were best suited producing these larger machines.

EARLY PRODUCT LINE

By 1894, Bucyrus had sold 171 shovels, gaining a solid reputation as a high-quality excavator producer. From 1895 through 1901, a total of twelve different sizes of steam shovels were offered, ranging from a 12-ton (11-tonne) model to a gigantic 95-ton (86-tonne) machine for use in mining and heavy railroad excavation. All of these were the partial-swing, Railroad type of shovel mounted on standard gauge railroad tracks.

The Gamboa was one of two 15-yard dipper dredges shipped to the Panama Canal Commission in 1913. These and other huge dipper dredges shipped by the company until 1930 represented the largest shovel dippers employed on any machine. They featured long dipper handles and cable- or rack-operated vertical spuds to hold position while digging.

This 13-foot placer dredge was shipped to Thailand for tin mining in 1929. Bucyrus had become a world leader in dredge manufacture by 1900 and many innovations in dredge design were incorporated into machines built up to World War II. Dredge orders then diminished, and the company sold its dredge interests to Ellicott Machine Company in 1953.

In 1910, Bucyrus entered the dragline market when it purchased manufacturing rights for the Heyworth-Newman dragline excavator. This steam-powered machine was mounted on skids and rollers and pulled itself along by its drag bucket. Bucyrus developed its successful Class-series draglines from this design.

Although some members of the company's management thought Bucyrus should compete in the "small" machine market, the developing trend during those years was toward larger machines. Of the 251 shovels sold, 219 weighed 45 tons (41 tonnes) or more. Of those, the 2 ½–cubic yard (1.9-cubic meter) shovel was by far the most popular. Designed by chief engineer A.W. Robinson in 1897 as a 60-ton (54-tonne) machine, it was redesigned as a 65-ton (59-tonne) machine the following year. Sales of that model alone totaled 138 units during the period between 1895 and 1901.

Bucyrus shovels were known for their robust strength and substantial construction. The company replaced cast iron in earlier models with cast steel, a much tougher material. The big shovels' construction included a base plate, a solid steel casting located at the front end of the car that extended its entire width. The lugs for attaching the A–frame and stabilizer arms were cast integral with the base plate, so that it bound the whole front end of the car together. This casting combined several parts into one piece, which were made separately in other shovels and often worked loose during operation. Independent thrusting (crowding) engines were added to the 65-ton (59-tonne) shovel in 1898 and,

in 1901, independent slewing engines were added so that the machine was equipped with separate power for each of the three basic motions.

The success of the 65-ton (59-tonne) shovel led Bucyrus to design even larger shovels and, after much hesitation, the construction of 75-ton (68-tonne), 85-ton (77-tonne), and 95-ton (86-tonne) machines was undertaken in 1899. The 95-ton (86-tonne) model was advertised as the most powerful shovel ever built and was equipped with a 5-cubic yard (3.8-cubic meter) dipper. Sixteen of these were sold during the first two years of its production, nine to railroads and the rest to mining companies in the rapidly expanding open pit mining operations on the Mesabi Range in Minnesota.

Steam shovels were not the only product of The Bucyrus Company in the early years. The vast array of products included railroad wrecking cars, ballast unloaders and spreaders, steam pile drivers, mine cars, and dredges. In 1883, Bucyrus shipped its first dipper dredge, and for seven decades dredges played a significant part in the company's history.

By 1890, Bucyrus had built several dipper dredges and added elevator (ladder type) dredges and hydraulic cutter dredges to its roster. By 1900, the

The Class 14 was the first Bucyrus excavator of any type to be equipped with crawler tracks. Appearing in 1912, the first sets consisted of hardwood shoes bolted on a simple chain belt. The Class 14 moved on four sets of crawlers and dug with a 2-yard bucket.

Bucyrus purchased a major competitor, the Vulcan Steam Shovel Company of Toledo, Ohio, in 1910. Excavators had been built at the Toledo plant since 1872 and Bucyrus gained some useful designs, including a fully-revolving shovel. The traction-wheel mounted Baby Giant shown here was one of Vulcan's smaller models.

company had built dipper dredges up to 7 cubic yards (5.4 cubic meters), elevator dredges weighing up to 225 tons (204 tonnes), and hydraulic dredges with twin 15-inch (38-centimeter) suction pumps. These were all monster machines in their day and helped Bucyrus become a world leader in that specialized field.

THE PANAMA CANAL

Bucyrus' reputation continued to grow as the company participated in major excavation projects across the United States and around the globe. Twenty-four Bucyrus shovels were used to dig the Chicago Drainage Canal and more were shipped to the vast open pit Mesabi Iron Range. Bucyrus dredges were shipped to the California gold fields and used in the enlargement of the New York State Barge Canal, the largest earth-moving project in the United States between 1902 and 1912. It was also during this time that mining overtook railroad building as the major market for large-sized shovels. The most prestigious project of all, though, was the Panama Canal.

The Bucyrus Company's early experience in building giant, heavy-duty shovels in the years leading up to America's involvement in the Panama Canal no doubt played a significant role in the company's success in supplying large numbers of machines to this massive project. One of the largest excavation projects of the early twentieth century, the Canal eventually involved excavation of over 300 million cubic yards (229 million cubic meters) of material, including some 50 million during the French effort that was aborted in 1888.

When America took over the Canal in 1904, no time was wasted in getting the excavation work started again. Bucyrus' management watched the situation and the opportunity develop with keen interest. Company vice-president S. L. G. Knox even visited the Panama site just prior to the company receiving its first shovel order in August 1904. The first order consisted of one 70-ton (64-tonne) and two 95-ton (86-tonne) shovels. When these shovels proved their merit, the Isthmanian Canal Commission quickly invited bids for eleven more machines, and Bucyrus was awarded the order.

The Atlantic Equipment Company was consolidated into the Bucyrus group in 1911. As a division of the American Locomotive Company, Atlantic was established in 1902 and had gained a fine reputation for railroad-type shovels, which excelled in hard rock mining. The shovels were distinguished by their massive boom structure and heavy-duty proportions as this picture shows.

President Theodore Roosevelt climbed aboard this 95-ton Bucyrus shovel during his inspection tour of the Panama Canal in 1908. Bucyrus delivered no fewer than 77 steam shovels to this prestigious project.

The Commission then began a series of bids for shovels in rapid succession as the excavation rate ramped up to full production. At one point in 1905, with 28 machines already on order, the Commission sent another inquiry to Bucyrus for 12 to 36 more shovels. Director E. K. Swigart responded in utter amazement by suggesting to the Commission that they didn't realize what had already been ordered. But the inquiry was correct, and Bucyrus was again successful in obtaining the orders.

Bucyrus' chief competitor in the Panama Canal bidding was the Marion Steam Shovel Company of Marion, Ohio. This would be one of many rival activities between the two companies over their respective long histories. By the time the Commission had ordered 61 shovels from Bucyrus, none had been supplied by any competitor, and the Bucyrus shovels were reported to have performed to the complete satisfaction of the Commission. When the next bid was announced for a further 28 shovels, the situation aroused aggressive action by Marion, who induced the Secretary of War, William Howard Taft, to intervene. Even though Bucyrus' tender was slightly lower than Marion's, Taft caused the Isthmanian Canal Commission to divide the order between

the two companies, citing that "the Government's interest requires an on–site comparison of competitive machines."

By the time the last shovel was shipped to Panama in 1908, a total of 102 had been delivered: 77 from Bucyrus, 24 from Marion, and a single shovel from the Thew Shovel Company. During this period, the shovels sold by Bucyrus to the Isthmanian Canal Commission constituted about one third of the total number of large shovels (70 tons [64 tonnes] and larger) sold by the company. Such extensive orders for similar products benefited Bucyrus in several ways. The certainty and size of the repetitive orders stimulated plant expansion and permitted the Company to famil-iarize itself with the economics of producing machines in large lots. The perfection of the 95-ton (86-tonne) shovel enabled Bucyrus to effectively challenge Marion's leadership in the large shovel field. But perhaps the most significant benefit was the substantial publicity the Company gained by its important contribution to the Canal construction, an advantage that has persisted in advertising to the present day. In 1908, former U.S. President Theodore Roosevelt climbed aboard a Bucyrus 95-ton (86-tonne) shovel on an inspection trip to the Canal. Six years later, the Canal opened, and a link between the Atlantic and Pacific oceans was established for ocean-going ships.

Bucyrus developed the industry's first revolving quarry and mine shovel, the 120-B, in 1925. It was joined the following year by the smaller 100-B shovel of 3 ½-yard capacity, depicted here in a steam version loading railroad cars. These early mining shovels featured rack-and-pinion type crowd, and gear drive to the lower works.

The Bucyrus-Monighan 15-W was one of the largest draglines to use clutches and brakes to transmit power to the hoist and drag drums instead of directly coupling them to electric motors. Only three were built in 1940, with booms up to 215 feet carrying buckets from 12 to 14 cubic yards.

BUCYRUS SUCCESSFULLY ENTERS THE DRAGLINE MARKET

The dragline excavator was introduced to the world by a number of drainage contractors in the Chicago area beginning in 1904. The specialist work was beyond the capability of steam shovels, which must work at the foot of the excavation. The contractors needed a machine that could stand on the surface, dig below its own level, and dump the material well clear of the working area, so some built their own machines. One of those contractor–builders, James O. Heyworth, approached Bucyrus in 1910 with an offer to sell manufacturing rights to his machine known as the Heyworth-Newman Dragline Excavator, of which several had been built and were operating successfully. Bucyrus management looked favorably on this proposal and stated, "The dragline type of machine will be one of vital importance in our line of manufacture, and it should make serious inroads upon the steam shovel business."

In 1910, Bucyrus entered the dragline market through the purchase of manufacturing rights for the Heyworth-Newman Dragline Excavator. The following year, Bucyrus introduced the Class 24 as the world's largest dragline. It was steam powered and carried a 3 ½–cubic yard (2.7–cubic meter) bucket on a 100-foot (30-meter) boom. The Class 14 dragline was introduced the following year as the first crawler-mounted dragline. Over 370 of the Class series draglines were produced from 1911 to 1937. They were offered with steam, gasoline, diesel, or electric power and could be mounted on rails, skids and rollers, or crawler tracks.

A close cousin to the dragline, the tower excavator, was introduced in 1915. Specifically designed for construction of levees along the lower Mississippi River, the tower excavator consisted of a head tower and tail tower positioned at opposite sides of the excavation with a slackline cableway system strung between them. A dragline bucket was suspended from a carriage that could travel a great distance across the excavation. Thirty-three tower excavators were built, and a number found use in open pit mines.

Bucyrus acquired a majority interest in the Monighan Machine Company of Chicago in 1931. Monighan draglines, with their unique walking devices, were considered superior to any other type of dragline on the market. The walking system was invented by Oscar Martinson of Monighan in 1913. A model 1-T is shown with the early chain-suspended shoes.

COMPANY EXPANSION AND PIVOTAL MERGERS

During the early years of the twentieth century, The Bucyrus Company was extremely interested in expanding and broadening its manufacturing base beyond a single plant. One avenue explored, which resulted in only marginal success, was the establishment of manufacturing affiliates in foreign countries to avoid their import tariffs. The first affiliate, Poutilov Works of St. Petersburg, Russia, commenced in 1900 and lasted until 1910. Up to that date, twelve large dredges and five of the largest steam shovels had been built to Bucyrus designs. After 1910, the manufacturing arrangement continued

Following the merging of Bucyrus and Monighan interests, the Bucyrus-Monighan Company was established in 1934. Martinson improved on his walking device in 1925 and launched the first of the new W series, the 2-yard 2-W, in 1926. This model remained in production until 1938, by which time walking draglines up to 10 cubic yards were being built.

No. 25 Special Overhead Spudding Machine

by tacit agreement only and came to an end at the outbreak of the Russian Revolution in 1917. Another manufacturing affiliate was established with the Canada Foundry Company of Toronto in 1904, but the Canadian company experienced considerable difficulty in manufacturing satisfactory machines because they lacked the quality and reliability of their American-built counterparts. With the good name of Bucyrus at stake, Company president H. P. Eells attempted to cancel the arrangement in 1909 by cutting off the supply of drawings and patterns, but Canada Foundry continued to build a few more "Canadian-Bucyrus" machines.

With the vigorous days of the Panama shovel orders over, new markets for the Company's products were opening up. In the first decade of the twentieth century, the shovel market was booming, but Bucyrus was missing out in several market areas, particularly in small excavators. The Company's chief competitors, Marion and Vulcan, began producing small fully revolving shovels in 1908. Bucyrus was lacking in manufacturing capacity; its sole South Milwaukee plant was more suited to produce dredge and large shovel equipment and was not easily adapted for building small revolving shovels. A survey of possible plant acquisitions was launched in 1909.

In 1910, Bucyrus took the opportunity to share in the purchase of a long-established competitor, the Vulcan Steam Shovel Company of Toledo, Ohio.

In 1933, Bucyrus-Erie entered the drill market by acquiring the manufacturing rights to the Armstrong Drill Company of Waterloo, Iowa. With roots going back to 1868, Armstrong had built up a well-respected line of mobile water well and oil well drills. This very early No. 25 Armstrong churn-type drill shows its wooden construction.

WATER WELL
WILLIAMS IOWA
DRILLED BY
J. J. BECKER FT. DODGE
IOWA
DEPTH 1743 ft
Nº 33
ARMSTRONG
ALL STEEL DRILL

The former Armstrong No. 33 drill (shown) became the Bucyrus-Armstrong 33-W water well drill, of which 243 were produced from 1933 to 1939. From these machines, Bucyrus developed a line of churn-type blasthole drills, which remained popular until the advent of the larger rotary drills in the early 1950s.

The Vulcan business was the successor of a number of enterprises that had used the Toledo plant to build excavating equipment, beginning in 1872 as the Toledo Foundry Machine Company. Vulcan's "Giant" line of steam shovels, which commenced in 1886, was moderately successful with the line extending to some of the largest at the time. In 1909, the Vulcan steam shovels ranged in size from 40 to 120 tons (36 to 109 tonnes). The forward-looking company had already produced small wheel-mounted excavators, pioneered electric drive on a mining shovel in 1899, and built a number of long-boom, railroad-type stripping shovels for surface mining. With the apparent perfect fit of the two companies' product lines and the fact that Vulcan had already headhunted a large number of former key Bucyrus personnel in an effort to stay competitive, an agreement was finalized to establish the Bucyrus-Vulcan Company.

Before Bucyrus and Vulcan came together, the latter had received a proposal from an industrial group in Evansville, Indiana, with a financial incentive to move its manufacturing operations to a 70-acre (28-hectare) site in that city

The 29-T churn-type drill acquired from the former Armstrong line turned out to be the most popular blasthole drill ever produced by Bucyrus. Production lasted until 1959 with 753 being sold. With electric, gasoline, or diesel power units available up to 65 horsepower, the 29-T could drill holes up to 9 inches in diameter.

where a new plant would be built. Bucyrus management had taken this into consideration with its purchase of Vulcan and earmarked the new plant at Evansville for manufacture of small revolving shovels. They followed through with the arrangement, and an extensive new plant was constructed in haste. As early as the spring of 1912, pilot models of two newly designed small steam shovels, the 5/8 yard 14–B and 7/8 yard 18–B, were ready for testing. These were the first products built at Evansville and the first revolving shovels to carry the Bucyrus name. Meanwhile, the former Vulcan line of shovels was discontinued and the remaining inventory sold off.

The Bucyrus–Vulcan Company established in 1910 was short-lived, as the following year another competitor, the Atlantic Equipment Company, was consolidated into the group. Atlantic, owned by the American Locomotive Company, was established in 1902 and had already gained a fine reputation for building heavy-duty railroad-type steam shovels that had made a name for themselves in hard rock mining. They were designed by A. W. Robinson, former chief engineer at Bucyrus. With the merger of Bucyrus, Vulcan, and Atlantic, the new corporate name became simply "Bucyrus Company," a public corporation, to distinguish it from The Bucyrus Company for legal purposes without losing the good will attached to the former name. This also marked the end of the Bucyrus organization as a family corporation.

This aerial shot shows the Evansville, Indiana, plant in its later years. Bucyrus Company built the plant and commenced manufacturing there in 1912. Mainly assigned to building the construction division's excavators up to the 88-B model, the plant also assisted with World War I British Government shell contracts and with mining machine component manufacture in the 1970s.

BUCYRUS DURING WORLD WAR I

Startup of the Evansville plant in 1912 did not go as well as expected. A newly hired and largely unskilled workforce, warranty work on shovels in the field, and a softening shovel market contributed to the problems. Even the introduction of three larger revolving shovels, the 1 ¼–cubic yard (1–cubic meter) 25-B, the 1 ½–cubic yard (1.2–cubic meter) 27-D skimmer, and the 1 ½–cubic yard (1.2–cubic meter) 35-B, along with manufacture of three dragline models transferred from South Milwaukee, failed to avoid financial losses for the first five years of operation. The result was the closing of the Evansville plant for 15 months. But the company persisted, and with successive changes in plant managers, improvements in manufacturing methods, and a boost from British government contracts during World War I, Evansville returned to profitability in 1916.

The British government contract that Bucyrus took on was for the supply of 8-inch (20-centimeter), high-explosive shells. After considerable reorganization and outlay for additional machine tools, production commenced at Evansville in 1916, reaching a peak rate of 16,000 shells per month. A portion of the British shell order and contracts for other special equipment were furnished from the South Milwaukee plant where further special machine tools had been installed. Bucyrus Company's special equipment and experience gained on the British contracts were useful in obtaining substantial orders for the American war effort. Equipment supplied to the U.S. government up to 1919 included 47 15-ton (14-tonne) locomotive cranes, 20 self-propelled derricks, and special forgings and components for 117 U.S. guns and 187 French guns.

POST WORLD WAR I TO 1927

The wartime contracts and postwar demand for small excavators helped the Evansville plant to operate profitably for several years, but another minor recession during 1921 and 1922 caused renewed losses. At this point, the Board of Directors considered transferring the Evansville operations to the South Milwaukee plant, which, in contrast, had remained profitable throughout the war period. The action to close the Evansville plant did not materialize, however, due to the insistence and foresight of President W. W. Coleman. Mr. Coleman initiated measures to raise the plant's efficiency and modernize its small shovel line, which had fallen behind in the competitive struggle.

In 1920, a significant machine was introduced, the 1-cubic yard crawler-mounted 30-B, Bucyrus' first universal excavator. "Universal" meant that the machine could be converted from the basic shovel to dragline, clamshell, or crane with minimal alteration to the machinery. The 30-B was initially a steam shovel, but a diesel engine was offered in 1921, making this the first diesel-driven shovel in the industry. An electric drive option appeared in 1922. That same year, the smaller 20-B and larger 50-B shovels, designed on lines similar to the 30-B, were unveiled. Along with the 30-B, these three successful excavators built at Evansville quickly displaced the pre-war Bucyrus small excavators. In the five years from 1923 through 1927, these models not only restored that plant's profitability to an acceptable level, but also accounted for 60 percent of total sales volume reported for small excavators during the 16-year history of the plant.

Rapid progress was being made in South Milwaukee with the introduction of several significant large mining machines. Undoubtedly the most noteworthy

The South Milwaukee plant as it appeared in 1927. Operations commenced here in 1893 after the company moved from its original location in Bucyrus, Ohio. It still serves as the company's main manufacturing plant and corporate headquarters with extensive modern additions over the years.

Designed by Lewis-Chambers Construction Company and built by Bucyrus-Erie in the 1930s, the Chambers Bridge was another machine first used in levee building on the Mississippi River. It was a crawler-mounted track-and-car system for transporting material from a dragline to the spoil bank. A 10-yard car made the return trip to the end of the 350-foot bridge in 50 seconds.

application of these was in the strip mining of bituminous coal. Between 1914 and 1927, the tonnage of coal produced by such methods expanded fourteen-fold, while the output from underground mines rose only 20 percent. There is no doubt the introduction of large shovels and draglines enabled such rapid expansion of surface mining, proving it to be the most efficient and low-cost method of mining where geological conditions permit.

Draglines, initially designed for drainage work and introduced by Bucyrus in 1910, were found entirely satisfactory in coal stripping operations where overburden was comparatively unconsolidated. In other areas, the stripping shovel was most advantageous because of its long reach, faster digging cycle, and capability of digging harder material. Bucyrus delivered its first stripping shovel, a 150–B with a 2 ½–cubic yard (1.9–cubic meter) dipper and 60-foot (18-meter) boom, in 1912. Larger machines followed, and by 1918, it was evident that an entire new industry had been created by the large, fully revolving shovel and dragline. Records show the company kept constant pace with the development of this important new market. By 1927, sizes of these machines had increased fivefold since inception and, as we now know, future machines would be built of a size beyond the wildest imagination of engineers at that time.

In 1925, Bucyrus introduced the 120-B quarry and mine shovel. This was a significant new class of machine because it was the first in the industry to combine the advantages of the fully revolving shovel with the proven heavy-duty digging capability of the part-swing railroad shovel. This machine was the forerunner of the present-day electric mining shovels, the development of which is covered in Chapter 2.

THE MERGER WITH ERIE—
SMALL SHOVEL MARKET DOMINATED

The roaring twenties produced a boom in construction work, and the small revolving excavator (1 cubic yard or under) led the way in mechanized excavation. Building basements needed to be dug; dirt roads were being graded and reconstructed for the motor age; and underground water, sewer, and other services were needed everywhere. These were the days before the crawler loader and loader-backhoe, before the wheeled loader had been perfected for excavation, and before the widespread use of hydraulics on construction equipment. Thus the "maid-of-all-work" fully revolving small cable excavator, with its array of attachments now including the backhoe, reigned as king of excavation for the next four decades. Consequently, a

In 1927, Bucyrus merged with the Erie Steam Shovel Company of Erie, Pennsylvania, to become the Bucyrus-Erie Company. The merger added a much-needed line of small fully-revolving shovels to Bucyrus' product line. Erie had been building steam shovels since 1914 and was America's leader in this field.

Bucyrus-Erie became a major supplier of tractor equipment to International Harvester in 1935. Thousands of dozer blades, tractor-mounted winches, pull-type scrapers, dozer shovels, and pull-type rippers were produced for the military during World War II. This field of TD-18 and TD-14 crawler tractors with Bucyrus-Erie attachments awaits shipment overseas.

multitude of manufacturers entered this market during the 1920s, and since most of these specialized in small machines, they rapidly overtook Bucyrus' market sales volume in this sector. By 1927, the small machine market was dominated (in order of size) by the Erie Steam Shovel Company, Northwest Engineering Company, and the Thew Shovel Company.

Bucyrus was well aware of its diminishing market share in the small machine category. In the early 1920s, it had introduced new "small" machines, the 20-B, 30-B, and 50-B, at Evansville in an attempt to rectify the problem. Sales of these machines were satisfactory and the heavy-duty 60-ton (54-tonne) 50-B was very popular, but it was not the machine for the small contractor who perhaps moved his machine several times a week completing small excavating jobs around town.

In 1927, Bucyrus merged with America's leader in small shovels, the Erie Steam Shovel Company of Erie, Pennsylvania, and a new corporate identity

emerged. A description of the newly named Bucyrus-Erie Company appeared on the New York Stock Exchange. Its focus was " . . . to bring together under one management, manufacturing plants, the products of which naturally supplement one another in the field of excavating machinery, by establishing a company handling power shovels, and other machinery for excavating and handling materials, of a number of sizes with the ability to sell these products with increased economy and efficiency, especially in foreign markets."

The Erie Steam Shovel Company began as the Ball Engine Company in 1883 as a manufacturer of steam engines and built its first steam shovel in 1914. It changed its name in 1922 to reflect its specialization in steam shovels. Undoubtedly, Erie's success was in no small part attributed to its intensive advertising in sales literature, magazines and its very aggressive sales policy. By concentrating on a very narrow size range, largely the ½–cubic yard Erie A and the ¾–cubic yard Erie B, sales efforts were simplified and low prices could be offered through streamlined manufacturing. The merger gave Bucyrus-Erie Company a strong presence in the small machine market and an additional major manufacturing plant at Erie, Pennsylvania, which would be devoted to the small construction size excavators.

The patented Dozer Shovel, designed for International TD-6 and TD-9 tractors, became standard Marine equipment in World War II. This one is unloading bombs in the Marshall Islands, South Pacific. Interchangeable buckets and blades equipped it to serve either as bulldozer or crawler loader. Power crowd was not provided for the bucket, and dumping was achieved by spring latch release.

Ruston-Bucyrus plant, Lincoln, England.

THE MERGER WITH RUSTON— WORLDWIDE MARKETING FORCE CREATED

Looking to the worldwide scene and potential increased export markets, Bucyrus-Erie joined with Ruston & Hornsby, Ltd., the foremost company in the British excavating machinery industry, to form Ruston-Bucyrus, Ltd. Ownership was split almost equally between the two companies. With its factory in Lincoln, England, Ruston & Hornsby, Ltd. and its predecessors had been building steam shovels since 1874. It was the only company outside the United States offering a full line of excavators of all sizes, including the giant stripping shovels and draglines that competed in size with those offered by Bucyrus and Marion. Earlier products included steam traction engines, pumps, oilfield equipment, steamrollers, and locomotives. Over 70 Ruston steam shovels were employed on the Manchester Ship Canal in England beginning in 1887. Over the following six years, 54 million cubic yards (41 million cubic meters) of material were moved on this project, the first ever to use powered excavators in considerable numbers.

After the merger, Ruston-Bucyrus consolidated the excavator lines of both companies. With free access to all Bucyrus-Erie designs, the Ruston models were gradually replaced with American designs. The merger also enabled Bucyrus-Erie to expand internationally; Ruston-Bucyrus acted as sales agents for those Bucyrus models not made in Lincoln, opening markets in countries where Bucyrus had previously been inactive.

The 480-W was a mid-size walking dragline with a long production run was. The 17-yard machine served a wide variety of mineral extraction industries including coal, bauxite, tin, oilsand, cement, copper, and clay, as well as major canal construction projects. Shipped to over a dozen countries from 1955 to 1979, many are still working today.

ENTER THE WALKING DRAGLINE

As noted previously, the Bucyrus Company entered the dragline market in 1910. Hundreds were sold over the next two decades and successfully operated on drainage projects and in surface mines. Some monster machines of the 1920s were able to convert from dragline to shovel and weighed up to 500 tons (454 tonnes). However, none of these were "walking" draglines. The draglines were mounted on skids and rollers on crawlers, or on rail trucks for running on one or more standard-gauge rail tracks, with their obvious restriction in mobility. Moving them involved a sizeable ground crew and prolonged costly downtime.

The Monighan Manufacturing Corporation of Chicago, Illinois, had been making walking draglines since 1913 with a unique propel system patented by their chief engineer, Oscar Martinson. The ingenious and simple device consisted of a pair of large shoes, one on each side of the machine, which moved in unison to raise and propel the machine in a walking motion. This freedom from rail tracks or skids and rollers was an obvious advantage to contractors, who increasingly chose the walking dragline over other types of propulsion. Well aware of the situation, Bucyrus-Erie purchased an interest in the Monighan Manufacturing Corporation in 1931, and followed through with further share purchases until 1934, when it gained full control of the company and changed its corporate name to the Bucyrus–Monighan Company. Oscar Martinson was named president.

Based on the 950-B shovels and draglines of the 1930s, the first Bucyrus-Erie 1150-B was launched in 1944. With buckets ranging from 20 to 25 cubic yards (15 to 19 cubic meters) and weighing 1,200 tons (1,089 tonnes), the 1150-B laid the foundation for larger draglines in the following decades.

The Monighan company had achieved profitability in every year since its existence, including through the depths of the Great Depression in the early 1930s, and its machines were held in high regard by its customers. At the time of the takeover, Monighan was one of only two companies in the world producing walking draglines. Page Engineering Company, also of Chicago, was the other. The Bucyrus-Monighan Company, with its Chicago plant, functioned as an independent unit until 1949 when Martinson retired as president and Bucyrus-Erie exercised overall control of the company. The plant finally closed in 1958, and walking dragline manufacture transferred to South Milwaukee.

ARMSTRONG DRILL COMPANY JOINS THE FAMILY

In 1933, Bucyrus-Erie entered the drill market by acquiring the manufacturing rights to the Armstrong Drill Company of Waterloo, Iowa. Armstrong could trace its manufacturing roots back to 1868 and offered a line of modern and well-respected oil well, water well, and blasthole mobile drills; bit dressers; and drill tools. They were well suited to Bucyrus-Erie's existing customers who were often involved with rock excavation that required blasting before it could be excavated. So the drill product line was easily sold and serviced through Bucyrus-Erie's existing organization. The drills were sold as Bucyrus-Armstrong products under a royalty agreement from 1933 to 1943, and thereafter as Bucyrus-Erie products. Today, blasthole drills are one of the company's three key products, along with shovels and walking draglines.

In 1946, Bucyrus-Erie developed the 42-T, the first Bucyrus churn drill with hydraulic leveling jacks. The product line was successful beyond imagination. 11,600 churn drills were sold up to 1984, many of them still in worldwide use today. In 1952, Bucyrus-Erie introduced the 50-R, the first commercially accepted large diameter rotary blasthole drill used in the mining industry. The 50-R was the first of over 1,350 rotary blasthole drills to be produced by Bucyrus. The 50-R achieved national fame in 1963, when it was instrumental in rescuing two trapped coal miners in the underground Sheppton Mine at Hazelton, Pennsylvania. This machine, normally used to drill 12 1/4-inch (31-centimeter) holes 100 feet (30 meters) deep, produced an 18-inch (46-centimeter), 330-foot (101-meter), deep rescue hole.

In the 1960s, new explosives requiring larger drill holes were introduced in the mining industry. The 45-R and 60-R drill models were developed to meet this need. The larger, more efficiently produced blast holes, combined with the more effective blasting agents, resulted in greater blasting productivity. These drills are covered in more detail in Chapter 4.

TRACTOR EQUIPMENT

Another product taken up by Bucyrus-Erie in the 1930s was crawler tractor attachments. Although the Bucyrus-Monighan and Bucyrus-Armstrong divisions were contributing earnings for the company during these Depression days, the big plants at South Milwaukee, Erie, and Evansville were operating at about one-third of capacity. Powerful diesel-powered crawler tractors were coming on the scene. When these machines were coupled to a pull-type scraper, contractors found they could move certain classes of material much cheaper than with traditional shovels and trucks. With a number of reported potential shovel sales losing out to tractors and scrapers, Bucyrus-Erie desired a piece of the action that would also help to fill its spare manufacturing space. It entered into discussion with International Harvester, a leading builder of crawler tractors. International was planning to expand its manufacturing capacity but did not desire to produce allied equipment. International's management considered Bucyrus-Erie's experience in manufacturing earthmoving equipment, its reputation in the field major advantages, and, that International's dealers would be pleased to have a reliable source of supply.

These discussions culminated in 1935 when Bucyrus-Erie President W. W. Coleman formally announced that the company would enter the new line of manufacture. He stated, "This type of machinery is performing the functions formerly done by excavators and, unless we enter into its manufacture, we can only look forward to a decrease in the sale of our present line for road construction work." As a result, Bucyrus-Erie became the major supplier of tractor equipment to International Harvester. The two companies' engineers worked closely together to design attachments for new tractor models before they were launched. Equipment supplied included two-wheel and four-wheel scrapers, cable winches, rippers, dozer blades, and crawler loaders.

By 1939, total annual shipments of the new products added during the 1930s climbed to 50 percent of the company's older lines. Manufacture of these products during World War II proved a great asset to the company as thousands were shipped worldwide to the Allied armed forces.

Bucyrus-Erie continued producing tractor equipment for a few years after the war, but in 1953 International Harvester announced it intended to produce its own allied equipment commencing in 1954. Consequently, after some 20 profitable years as a tractor allied equipment builder, Bucyrus-Erie agreed to phase out these products.

BUCYRUS-ERIE IN WORLD WAR II

With the outbreak of World War II, Bucyrus-Erie experienced an increased demand for its excavators. The company was fortunate in not having to re-tool for new products to any great extent. For the most part, the government wanted its standard products. This allowed Bucyrus to fulfill its government contracts with basically standard products while upgrading them for later civilian use. Bucyrus also produced special ordinance equipment, specifically gun carriages. In the war years 1942 to 1945, some two-thirds of the company's production was devoted to the war effort. Its small excavators sold in large quantities to the armed forces. The ½–cubic yard 15-B universal excavator was the most popular, often selling complete with a number of front end attachments.

An interesting insight into the Bucyrus-Erie's management philosophy can be gained from the fact that, with the exception of the gun carriages, the company refused to expand its plant to accommodate additional orders for special equipment, preferring to increase production of its standard products within its existing manufacturing facilities. In 1942, for example, it indicated that it was not interested in supervising the construction and operation of a government-financed tank factory at South Milwaukee. In making the decision not to expand at a time when the U.S. States government was willing to finance additional facilities, the company indicated that it was looking ahead to the period when excess manufacturing capacity might accompany a recession, as experience had shown following World War I.

In 1962, the first Bucyrus-Erie 3850-B stripping shovel went to work at Peabody Coal Company's Sinclair Mine in Kentucky. Its 115-yard (88-cubic meter) dipper was almost double the size of any then in operation! Two years later, Peabody put another 3850-B to work with a slightly shorter boom and 140-yard dipper. These were the largest shovels ever built by Bucyrus.

The 3850-Bs were manufactured in the South Milwaukee plant and shipped to their destinations in over 300 railcars. The shovels were supported on four two-crawler propelling assemblies, each carrying a 54-inch (137-centimeter) diameter hydraulic cylinder to support and level the machine. One of the massive cylinders is shown being manufactured in South Milwaukee.

When increased production following the war was assured, Bucyrus invested $2 million in an expansion program that increased plant capacity. Through the purchase of other companies and their patents, Bucyrus continued to expand its product line to include contractor-size cranes and excavators and all-hydraulic truck cranes.

HYDROCRANE—
FORERUNNER OF THE HYDRAULIC EXCAVATOR

In 1948, an interesting new type of excavator/crane attracted the attention of Bucyrus-Erie management. This was a truck-mounted hydraulic crane with a telescopic boom and hydraulically-operated outriggers. Named the H-2 Hydrocrane by its inventor, Roy O. Billings, president of the Milwaukee Hydraulics Corporation, it was put into production by his firm in 1946. As one of America's first-ever hydraulic cranes, it was a very simple and highly mobile machine that became an instant success with some 200 sold by the end of the following year.

THE GEM OF EGYPT

On examination, Bucyrus-Erie's chief engineer, G. Y. Anderson, commended the machine's simplicity, safety, and mobility. He noted the machine's hydraulic outriggers and jacks, which could be "set so quickly and easily that they are always used, saving the truck and tires, and giving the light-weight unit remarkable stability." Accordingly, Bucyrus-Erie purchased the Milwaukee Hydraulics Corporation in 1948, a move that would be significant for the company in later years. It was Bucyrus-Erie's first move into hydraulic machines and paved the way for a full line of hydraulic excavators that would sell in large numbers in the 1960s and 1970s. It also sowed the seed for what would become an extensive line of Bucyrus-Erie hydraulic truck cranes with capacities of up to 110 tons (100 tonnes). The truck-mounted Hydrocrane product—and the backhoe version, the Hydrohoe—was upgraded over the years and would remain in Bucyrus-Erie's product line until 1981.

DREDGES AND BUCKET WHEELS

Dredges formed a significant part of Bucyrus' business in the early years. The period from 1889 to 1910 was the most prolific for dredge manufacture, when the company shipped an average of 12 dredges each year. After that time, dredge shipments leveled out to three or four per year up to World War II, but the variety and size of machines increased during that period. Most

Bucyrus-Erie's final stripping shovels were two 1950-Bs purchased by the Hanna Coal Company (now Consolidation Coal Company) for coal stripping in southeastern Ohio. The second of these was the Gem of Egypt, which started work in 1967. Boom length was 170 feet (52-meters) and its dipper held 130 cubic yards (99 cubic meters). Operating weight was 6,850 tons (6,214 tonnes).

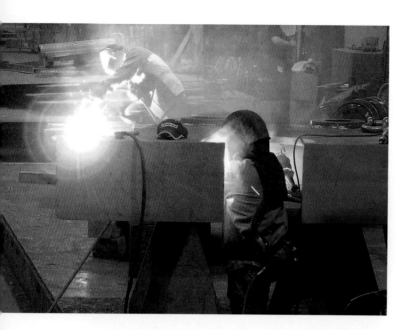

Assembling a large excavator demands a huge amount of welding. Here a welder works on a large component in the South Milwaukee plant. The components are made as large as possible for economy but small enough to be shipped. The components are finally assembled and welded together at the erection site.

notable were two huge dipper dredges, the Mogul and the Crest, built for the Great Lakes Dredge & Dock Company. The Crest, built in 1925, held the world record with its 16-cubic yard (12-cubic meter) dipper as the largest mounted on any excavating machine at that time. These two floating monsters served their owners well for over half a century.

After World War II, dredge orders dwindled, and only five more were sold up to 1950 when the last, a 15-inch (38-centimeter) hydraulic diesel type was shipped to Finland. The longevity of the machines and a decrease in gold dredging contributed to the market saturation. Bucyrus-Erie officially withdrew from the market in 1953, and the dredge business was sold in 1957.

Another specialized machine built by Bucyrus-Erie was the bucket wheel excavator. Unlike those built in Europe where the continuous flow of material is transferred onto a transfer bridge and conveyor system, the Bucyrus-Erie wheel type was a self-contained outfit known as a cross-pit wheel. It was designed of large dimensions to enable it to dig from the high wall of a surface coal mine and discharge onto the spoil pile in one continuous operation. The digging wheel, transfer conveyor, machinery house, and discharge conveyor were part of a revolving superstructure mounted on a crawler-propelled base. The first of these wheel excavators was developed by the United Electric Coal Company of Chicago beginning in 1943. The efficiency and high output of the machine attracted Bucyrus-Erie's interest, and a cooperative development arrangement was made between the two companies. United Electric eventually built five of these lumbering giants, utilizing the crawler-propelled lower works salvaged from former stripping shovels.

In 1954, the Truax-Traer Coal Company of Chicago put into operation the Bucyrus-Erie 954-WX, a machine designed as a wheel excavator from the crawlers upward. The company sold a few more cross-pit wheel excavators in this small market restricted by geological conditions. Then, in 1986, the latest and largest was commissioned at the Captain Mine in Illinois (see page 54).

ERA OF GIANT STRIPPING MACHINES

The boom in coal-fired power generation in the 1950s produced a demand for stripping machines larger than any previously built. Bucyrus-Erie responded by designing and building the 55-cubic yard (42-cubic meter) 1650-B stripping shovel. The 2,450-ton (2,223-tonne) monster known as the River Queen went to work for Peabody Coal Company in 1956. By the end of the decade, both Bucyrus-Erie and competitor Marion Power Shovel Company placed a number of large stripping shovels in the Midwestern coal fields.

With experience gained from these machines, Bucyrus-Erie took the spotlight in 1960 when it announced it had secured an order from Peabody Coal Company for the world's largest shovel, a 3850-B stripping shovel with a dipper capacity of 115 cubic yards (88 cubic meters), almost double the size of the largest shovel then in operation! With a weight of over 9,000 tons (8,165 tonnes), the machine captured the public's attention as its progress was

Shown alongside a 10-B, Bucyrus-Erie's smallest excavator, the massive 950-B stripping shovel of 30–cubic yard capacity was the world's largest land machine in 1935. Weighing 1,250 tons, the 950-B embodied many innovations used on subsequent Bucyrus machines, such as a rope crowd with tubular dipper handle and a two-part boom.

Probably the most famous of all excavating machines is the 4250-W Big Muskie, the world's largest dragline. Swinging a bucket of 220 cubic yards (168 cubic meters) on a 310-foot (94-meter) boom, and weighing 14,500 tons (13,154 tonnes), Big Muskie is regarded as one of the engineering marvels of the twentieth century.

reported in stories around the world. Before the first 3850-B went to work in 1962, Peabody ordered a second similar machine, this time with a 140-cubic yard (107-cubic meter) bucket. Peabody's order for the second 3850-B without testing the first was a clear demonstration of its confidence that the Bucyrus-Erie design would perform as promised. The second 3850-B went to work in 1964 and remains the largest shovel ever built by the company.

A significant accomplishment was the manufacture of Big Muskie, the largest dragline ever built. Going to work in 1969, the one and only 220-cubic yard (168-cubic meter) Bucyrus-Erie 4250-W was one of the largest mobile earthmoving machines ever built. Estimated at 14,500 tons (13,154 tonnes) operating weight, the sheer magnitude of the dragline continues to amaze people. Nearly 22 stories high, with a length of about 460 feet (140 meters) and a bucket as large as a 12-car garage, the machine operated in the Muskingum mine in eastern Ohio until 1991. Although Big Muskie was scrapped in 1999, the bucket is currently on display in an Ohio recreation park.

CONTINUED SUCCESS

Expansion overseas continued in 1963 with joint ventures established in Japan, Brazil, and Australia. The following decades brought further success and increased product lines for Bucyrus. By 1971, net shipments were a record $185 million. That year, Bucyrus-Erie acquired the Hy-Dynamic Company of Lake Bluff, Illinois. This company was best known for its Dynahoe, a tractor-mounted combination loading shovel and hydraulic backhoe that became a Bucyrus-Erie product and remained in the line until 1985. Hy-Dynamic also provided Bucyrus-Erie with a line of rough-terrain, wheel-mounted hydraulic cranes to supplement its comprehensive construction equipment lines of hydraulic and cable excavators, truck cranes, and drills. On the mining front, Bucyrus-Erie introduced the 21-cubic yard (16-cubic meter) 295-B in 1972, its largest mining shovel to date. It was the first of a long line of big modern electric mining shovels that continue today in their updated form. During the 1970s, annual sales increased to over $750 million.

THE ARAB OIL EMBARGO

The Arab Oil Embargo of October 1973 caused worldwide panic at the prospect of running out of oil in the foreseeable future. The long lines at gasoline pumps in the United States brought home to the average American the country's critical dependency on foreign energy sources. In the energy industries, the obvious answer to a shortage of oil was to expand the use of coal as the most reliable and abundant source of energy for power generation. Domestic U.S. coal reserves were deemed adequate for hundreds of years of use. Consequently, plans for rapid expansion of coal mining were put in place as an emergency measure. Electric utilities moved to secure additional coal sources, and oil companies scrambled to purchase coal reserves. In many cases, the oil companies would develop their own mines.

Coal production expanded rapidly in the world energy arena. Countries such as the United States, Australia, Canada, and the United Kingdom that had well-established and mechanized surface coal mining industries were quick to order new surface mining equipment at an unprecedented rate. The United Kingdom doubled its opencast coal production during the 1970s. A few walking draglines were sold there, but the preferred equipment type was the large diesel-powered hydraulic excavator, a machine type not offered by Bucyrus-Erie. However, Ruston-Bucyrus, its U.K. affiliate, was successful in supplying the mining contractors with large numbers of electric mining shovels made at the Lincoln plant.

The world market for large walking draglines in the ten years before 1973 had averaged some 12 machines per year. Now, due to the sudden need for

A school band shows off the immensity of the 220–cubic yard (168–cubic meter) bucket of the Big Muskie dragline that began working in 1969 at the Central Ohio Coal Company's Muskingum Mine in Ohio. The bucket with contents weighed 550 tons (499 tonnes) and was suspended by four wire hoist ropes and four drag ropes, all 5 inches (13 centimeters) in diameter.

coal, the ongoing need for phosphate, and the regular expansion of mineral production throughout the world, the number of these machines needed in surface mining rose dramatically. This unprecedented worldwide demand created an overwhelming situation for Bucyrus-Erie, probably the most significant in its entire history and probably one unparalleled in any other industry.

By the end of 1973, the number of orders received by Bucyrus-Erie would require more than fifteen years to produce using its normal production capacity at maximum utilization. The backlog at year-end had shot up to $151 million, compared with $84 million a year earlier. By the end of 1974, the backlog would skyrocket to $636 million. This chaotic market situation was such that the company was able to return a large number of unexecuted dragline order contracts received in 1973, originally quoted on terms that would not allow adequate recovery of rapidly increasing costs. It was then able to renegotiate all these contracts at prices raised to cover higher material costs, a premium on imported steel—which could only be procured in sufficient quantities from foreign sources—increased sub-contract work, increased hiring and training of personnel, and expanded facilities needed to increase production. Customers with machines on order were even willing to pay a premium to move up the long backlog list and ensure delivery of their machine at the earliest opportunity. With no end in sight to the high level of incoming orders and prospects of the backlog rising even further during 1974, Bucyrus-Erie management chose to accept the challenge to fulfill all its incoming orders within a reasonable time frame instead of turning orders away.

A plan formulated at the beginning of 1974 moved the company into immediate action on several fronts. So vigorous was the activity that Bucyrus-Erie doubled its manufacturing space in less than a year. The South Milwaukee plant added machine tools and extended existing buildings. A machine shop and foundry were purchased at Glassport, Pennsylvania, with a potential capacity equal to that of the foundry at South Milwaukee. A new facility was purchased in Racine, Wisconsin, which manufactured electrical components and became the Central Parts Depot. Biggest of all was the purchase of a huge former Naval Ordnance plant at Pocatello, Idaho, with 1.4 million square feet (130,100 square meters) of manufacturing space under roof, more than the 1.2 million square feet (111,500 square meters) at South Milwaukee. Acquired in April, 1974, the Pocatello plant achieved its first shipments only two months later. Meanwhile, the Evansville and Erie plants, normally building only construction-sized machines, were modified to build mining machinery components as well. These expansions resulted in Bucyrus-Erie's manufacturing facilities rising from 2.3 million square feet (213,700 square meters) at the end of 1973 to 4.6 million square feet (427,400 square meters) just a year later.

In addition to plant expansions, the company initiated other activities to facilitate the building of mining equipment. Ruston-Bucyrus in England helped to fulfill Bucyrus-Erie orders for 480-W and 1260-W walking draglines, some of which were shipped to the United States. Local manufacture of certain dragline components was carried out for draglines ordered in Australia and

The Arab Oil Embargo of the early 1970s boosted the use of coal as the most reliable and abundant source of energy for power generation. In a typical western coal mining scene, this Bucyrus-Erie 1300-W dragline removes the relatively shallow overburden to expose a thick, low-sulfur coal seam, which is being loaded by a 295-B electric shovel.

South Africa, and affiliate Komatsu–Bucyrus in Japan built 195-B and 280-B mining shovels. Subcontract work for machine components also increased. The close of 1974 found the company in a race to meet commitments and utilize new capital, with doubled manufacturing space and a greatly expanded workforce in a crash program of expansion.

RECESSION IN THE 1980S

By 1975, the expanded facilities came into full production and Bucyrus-Erie enjoyed full use of these for about five years. During this period, backlog peaked at $681 million in 1975 and sales reached $547 million in 1977, but by the end of 1978 the backlog had somewhat declined due to a slow-down of new orders. The widely expected shift of electric utility fuel from oil to coal failed to materialize as governmental regulations either prevented it outright or made coal conversions uneconomical. Meanwhile, the traditional growth in electric power consumption slowed so that utilities were under lessened pressure to commit to any additional power plants, whatever the fuel might be. When the dust settled following the buying frenzy of the mid-1970s, coal producers began to cancel large numbers of orders. These were the first signs of a coming recession in the mining industry.

In 1974 Bucyrus-Erie purchased this large plant in Pocatello, Idaho, to cope with an unprecedented volume of mining machine orders. The extensive 1.4 million square foot plant, together with other company expansions, effectively doubled the company's manufacturing space within one year. Pocatello shipped mining machines for a nine year period until the recession of the 1980s.

This view shows the company's Erie, Pennsylvania, plant in 1972. The plant was home to the Erie Steam Shovel Company until 1927, when Bucyrus acquired this leader in small revolving shovels to become the Bucyrus-Erie Company. The plant served the company well until its closure in 1984.

The South Milwaukee facility, shown here in 1980, has been Bucyrus' headquarters and main manufacturing plant since 1893. The many different buildings have been added at different eras in the company's long history. The new corporate office is at the front, the machine testing area at the rear. Compare with 1927 view on page 30.

For a company used to the cyclic nature of the mining and construction industries, Bucyrus-Erie had been prepared to take corrective action when similar events occurred in the past. But the recession of the 1980s was more than most earthmoving equipment manufacturers could take. Great changes occurred across the industry, with bankruptcies, mergers, and takeovers being reported almost every month. Bucyrus-Erie did not escape the crippling recession but was able to survive by transforming itself into a company serving only the surface mining industry. The size of the company was drastically reduced, and all manufacturing was consolidated to its South Milwaukee plant.

Plants were sold successively, beginning with Glassport in 1981. Racine and Evansville went the following year. The Evansville Plant had been with the company since 1912. The massive Pocatello plant was vacated in 1983 after only nine years of production, and Erie was sold in 1984. Finally, in 1985, the company sold its share in Ruston-Bucyrus Ltd. Ruston-Bucyrus Ltd. continued to produce machines in England under new ownership and the new name of R-B Lincoln plc. All rights to Bucyrus-Erie's non-mining products, including truck cranes, offshore cranes, tractor-backhoes, and

construction-size hydraulic and cable excavators were either sold to other companies or discontinued by 1985. The remaining products, including electric shovels, walking draglines, and rotary blasthole drills, have become the company's main products and are continuously updated to serve the increasing needs of the surface mining industry.

ACHIEVEMENTS IN THE 1980S

In 1980, Bucyrus-Erie continued its long tradition of technology leadership by shipping the first electric mining shovel equipped with AC electric motors and controls. The 34-cubic yard (26-cubic meter) 395-B, with its innovative electrical design, heralded a new era for large excavators. Since then, continued innovations have kept Bucyrus at the forefront of electrical technology.

In an effort to counteract the cyclic nature of the mining equipment business, Bucyrus-Erie purchased Western Gear Corporation, a manufacturer of aerospace products, in 1981. To recognize this diversity, the company changed its name to Becor Western, Inc. in 1985, but the Bucyrus-Erie Company name was retained for its mining machinery division. Two years later, Western Gear Corporation was sold, and, in a leveraged buyout in 1988, the company was purchased by B-E Holdings, Inc., a group of private investors.

Bucyrus designed and built some giant cross-pit bucket-wheel excavators over the years, gaining valuable experience in this specialized field. In the right geological conditions, the wheel is the most efficient means of moving high volumes of material. This 1054-WX wheel boasted a telescopic digging boom and carried nine 1-yard buckets on the 24-foot diameter wheel.

The 5,380-ton 5872-WX cross-pit wheel excavator was commissioned in 1986 at the Captain Mine of Arch Coal Inc. This was the largest of its type ever built. Its 72-inch wide conveyor belt, moving at 1,200 feet per minute, could deliver material more than 720 feet from the digging face to the spoil pile. The 5872-WX was scrapped following the mine closure in 1998.

During the 1980s, the company's drilling line prospered. Two massive 67-Rs, the largest in the product line, were shipped to Australia. In 1986, the 49-R blasthole drill was ushered in.

As a special one-of-a-kind design, Bucyrus-Erie built the largest-ever cross-pit wheel excavator and placed it in service at the Captain Mine, Illinois, in 1986. Built on the base of a Marion 5860 stripping shovel, this 25-story monster was 716 feet (218 meters) long and weighed 5,380 tons (4,881 tonnes).

RANSOMES & RAPIER PURCHASED

Bucyrus-Erie continued its acquisition of key companies that would contribute to overall success in the dragline market. In 1988, it acquired the dragline assets of Ransomes & Rapier Ltd. of England, affording greater participation in the Indian market where most of their recent draglines had been sold.

Established in 1869, Ransomes & Rapier built an array of heavy equipment including locomotive cranes and large dockside cranes. Its name was well-known worldwide for many industry achievements, including the first locomotive to run in China (1874), the world's largest steam locomotive crane (120 tons [109 tonnes] at a 20-foot [6-meter] radius), a central concrete mixing plant in 1887, and water-control sluice gates for high profile waterways such as the Nile in Egypt; Lloyd Barrage at Sukkur, India; River Clyde in Scotland; and River Thames and Manchester Ship Canal in England. Ransomes & Rapier built its first excavator, a rail-mounted steam shovel, and shipped it to Australia in 1914. From 1924 to 1936, it built excavators under license from the Marion Steam Shovel Company, a company that would become part of the Bucyrus organization decades later.

A significant contributor to the history of walking dragline manufacture, Ransomes & Rapier had built its first dragline in 1939. In 1961, it placed in service the 40–cubic yard (31–cubic meter) Rapier W1800, the world's largest at that time. Bucyrus continues to market the Rapier design walking draglines with the primary sales continuing to be in India, where 15 are currently in operation and more are pending.

In 1988, Bucyrus acquired the design and manufacturing rights of the British dragline maker Ransomes & Rapier Ltd. Rapier's first walking dragline was this 4-yard W170 built in 1939. It featured the Cameron & Heath patented walking system utilizing an eccentric wheel running in a larger roller bearing, a feature of every subsequent Rapier dragline.

The former Rapier-designed W2000 dragline was retained as a Bucyrus product following the Ransomes & Rapier takeover in 1988. The 45-yard machine was popular in certain foreign countries, especially India, where some 15 units operate in coal mines. Rapier built the world's largest walking draglines throughout the 1950s.

A NEW NAME FOR THE 1990S

In 1990, Bucyrus was successful in placing a 2750WS at Black Thunder Mine in the United States. This 14-million pound (6,350,000-kilogram) dragline offered updated engineering designs throughout and introduced AC motors to large excavators. The 2750WS, with its 160–cubic yard (122–cubic meter) bucket, is currently the largest dragline operating in North America.

The latest entry into the drill product line is the unique 39HR. Its round mast tubes arranged in a triangular fashion form an inherently sound structure. The 59-R, used in taconite drilling operations, is the most powerful blasthole drill in current use.

Following financial difficulties in the early 1990s, the company went through a period under Chapter 11 bankruptcy protection from February 1993 to December 1994. It emerged after financial restructuring and returned to public ownership. In 1996, Bucyrus-Erie Company changed its name to Bucyrus International, Inc. to better reflect its international market with the highest percentage of its sales being shipped outside of the United States.

MARION POWER SHOVEL ACQUIRED—
113-YEAR RIVALRY ENDS

In 1997, with one of the greatest takeovers in excavator history, Bucyrus acquired Marion Power Shovel Company. This takeover of the second-largest dragline manufacturer in the business (Bucyrus being the largest) effectively ended an intense competitive rivalry between these two companies that lasted some 113 years. Marion had been established in 1880 as the Marion Steam Shovel & Dredge Company and grew into one of the fore-most manufacturers of excavating machines. Marion became a key player in providing giant stripping shovels to the coal industry, being the first to put a long-boom revolving stripping shovel to work in North America in 1911. Marion's succession of giant shovels, many breaking world size records, culminated in the world's largest in 1965. This behemoth, the Marion 6360 at the Captain Mine, Illinois, wielded a 180–cubic yard (138–cubic meter) dipper. With an estimated weight of 15,000 tons (13,600 tonnes), this machine still holds the record as the heaviest mobile land machine ever built. Marion entered the walking dragline business in 1939, and produced the largest dragline built at the time just three years later. In April 1946, the company changed its name to the Marion Power Shovel Company to more closely reflect its products.

Bucyrus purchased the Marion Power Shovel Company in 1997. In 1951, Marion had shipped the first 10–cubic yard (7.7–cubic meter) 191-M mining shovel, the largest on two crawlers at that time. The 191-M proved to be one of Marion's most popular shovels with 156 sold until 1989, by which time its capacity had been upped to 15 cubic yards (12 cubic meters).

One of Marion's first draglines was the model 7800, the world size record holder in 1942. The 30-yard machine remained in production for 22 years with 19 units being shipped. This picture shows the 7800 still operating at the Highvale Mine in Alberta, Canada. It is owned by TransAlta Utilities and operated by Luscar Ltd.

Marion also produced a line of large blasthole drills. The big M4 weighed up to 130 tons and exerted 105,000 pounds of pull-down force on the drill bit. Drilling holes up to 12 1/4 inches in diameter, the M4 could handle 55 feet of drill steel in one pass.

Over the years, Marion followed a similar path to Bucyrus by participating in strategic takeovers of significant companies to enhance its sales effort or product line. Acquisitions included the Osgood Company and its subsidiaries, the General Excavator Company and Commercial Steel Casting Company, both of Marion, Ohio, purchased in 1954, and the Quick Way Truck Shovel Company of Denver, Colorado, in 1961.

Marion made headlines when it built the famous Apollo moon rocket transporters for NASA in 1965. Based on stripping shovel undercarriage technology, the two diesel-electric transporters were designed to move fully assembled lunar spacecraft and rockets from the assembly building at Cape Canaveral to the launch pad, a distance of three miles. These huge vehicles weighing 3,000 tons (2,722 tonnes) without load are powered by six diesel generator sets generating 7,600 horsepower (5,667 kilowatts). Still in use today, the transporters have taken part in most of the major space programs including the Space Shuttle.

Marion unveiled the 301M electric mining shovel in 1986 with 57-yard dipper and operating weight of 1,150 tons. The technically advanced shovel featured planetary gear drives on all motions and DC static power conversion. In 1995, the 301M became the 351M with improved diagnostics and digital control, then it became the Bucyrus 595B following the Bucyrus takeover in 1997.

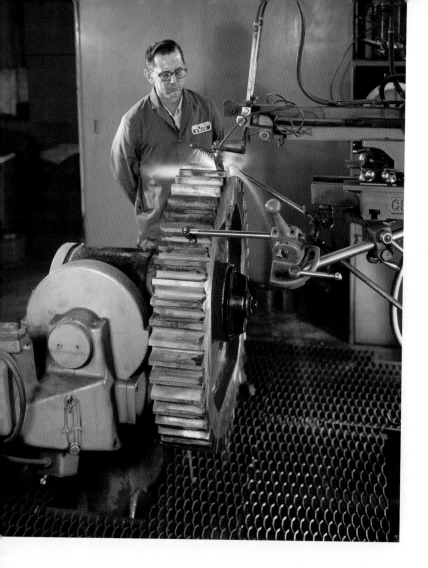

Top quality gearing has always been a priority at Bucyrus. The metallurgy must be exactly to specification. If too soft, the gear will wear prematurely; too hard, it could cause wear or extensive damage to the entire gear train. Heat treating is an important process. Here a gear is being induction hardened in the South Milwaukee plant.

INTERNATIONAL EXCAVATION EQUIPMENT LEADER

The Marion acquisition broadened Bucyrus' product line, adding over 120 operating draglines to its fleet and enabling Bucyrus to gain a wealth of technical data relative to design concepts and historical performance of its former chief competitor. Updated versions of some former Marion machines are now marketed under the Bucyrus banner. The reinforcement of the shovel product line with the Marion 351M (now the 595B), coupled with the existing successful 495-series shovels, places Bucyrus in an ideal position to satisfy future customer requirements.

During 1999 and 2000, Bucyrus produced the 2750WS dragline, which was shipped and erected in Australia. Weighing 8,000 tons (7,257 tonnes) and swinging a 156–cubic yard (119–cubic meter) bucket on a 360-foot (110-meter) boom, this is currently the world's largest operating dragline by virtue of its Rated Suspended Load (RSL) capability of 800,000 pounds (362,900 kilograms). Today's draglines are primarily stripping machines, removing great quantities of material to allow access to underlying coal and mineral deposits.

Bucyrus and its acquired companies have produced over 150,000 excavating machines since inception. The combined excavator design and manufacturing expertise totals more than 600 years. Since 1913, the Bucyrus family of companies has built a total of 1,320 walking draglines comprising more than 85 different models. The Bucyrus brands represent nearly 90 percent of the world's dragline population. Bucyrus is proud to celebrate 95 years of dragline manufacturing. The company has also produced over 13,200 drills since 1933.

With over 70 percent of sales and service performed overseas, Bucyrus International, Inc. has established itself as an international leader in excavation

equipment manufacturing. International subsidiaries are located within Africa, Australia, Brazil, Canada, Chile, China, Europe, India, and Peru. There are several locations throughout the United States as well.

MOVING FORWARD

Throughout company history, Bucyrus has led the industry in innovative products designed to satisfy some of the world's toughest earthmoving requirements. Research and development efforts continue to add new products and improve established product lines. Today, with 125 years of experience, Bucyrus continues to provide its worldwide surface mining customers with leading technology products, high-quality OEM parts, and dedicated service professionals to ensure optimal machine productivity and dependability.

The largest dragline currently operating in North America is this 2570WS owned by Thunder Basin Coal Company at its Black Thunder Mine in Wyoming. Its 675,000-pound suspended load capability enables it to work with a 160-yard bucket on a 335-foot boom. The 2570WS represents the very latest in Bucyrus dragline technology.

CHAPTER TWO

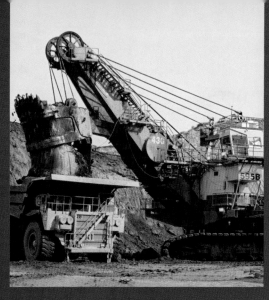

T. & O.C F

B44

SHOVELS

THE FIRST SHOVELS

The 1835 steam shovel, designed by William S. Otis and patented in 1839, is the earliest known single-bucket excavator for use on land. Otis was a partner in a firm of contractors who used their own machines for railroad construction. When Otis died of typhoid fever in 1839 at the early age of 26, the shovel patents were strictly held by the family contracting business for over 40 years. The idea of mechanized excavation caught on very slowly because manual labor was cheap and plentiful and steam shovels were consequently built in small numbers until the Otis patents finally expired in the late 1870s. At that point, several other companies in the United States began building steam railroad shovels as construction gained momentum. Most noteworthy were the Osgood Dredge Company of Troy, New York (1875); Vulcan Iron Works of Toledo, Ohio (1882); Marion Steam Shovel & Dredge Company of Marion, Ohio (1884); and Bucyrus Foundry & Manufacturing Company of Bucyrus, Ohio (1882). These companies are the founders of the American shovel manufacturing industry, and today their descendants all operate under the umbrella of Bucyrus International, Inc.

The earliest recorded application of a digging machine used in strip mining was in 1885, when coal mining contractors Wright & Wallace used a land

Opposite: This Thompson Iron Steam Shovel and Derrick was the first shovel built by the Bucyrus Foundry and Manufacturing Company. Designed by John Thompson, Manager of Manufacturing, the shovel was purchased in 1882 by the Toledo & Ohio Central Railroad. William S. Otis had built the first steam shovel in 1835, but closely held patents by the Otis family limited shovel development prior to the Thompson machine.

Bucyrus railroad shovels were designed for heavy-duty excavation and formed the backbone of the company's products in the early years. Because most of these limited swing machines worked on railroad construction, they became known as railroad shovels. But like this one owned by the Morgan Gold Mining Company in Australia, they were found to be ideally suited to hard rock mining.

dredge to strip coal at Mission Field near Danville, Illinois. The contractor bought an old dredge made of wood, removed the hull, and placed the machine on rollers. He installed a wooden boom 50 feet (15 metres) long and a dipper with a capacity of 1 ¼ cubic yards (1 cubic meter). Several similar land dredges were made before the turn of the century, but these wooden machines had very short working lives.

In 1899, Vulcan built two long-boom stripping shovels to mine phosphate for the Berkley Chemical Company. These successful machines were known as Vulcan Phosphate Specials, and seven more were built over a short period of time. Vulcan continued to build long-boom shovels for stripping applications. In 1907, a surface coal mining company fitted a long-boom on a Vulcan Model K part-swing railroad-type shovel and used it to strip overburden near Lily, Kentucky. The largest Vulcan stripper went to work near Tulsa, Oklahoma, in 1910. This was the Class L, a 130-ton (118-tonne), 2–cubic

yard (1.5–cubic meter) land dredge with a 60-foot (18-meter) boom. It was profitably used to strip 17 feet (5.2 meters) of overburden from a coal seam only two feet thick. Later that same year, Bucyrus purchased the Vulcan Steam Shovel Company and its designs.

All the above Vulcan machines and the earlier mining dredges were of the non-revolving type. They were designed on the railroad shovel principle, where the boom and dipper handle were capable of swinging only about 200 degrees instead of a full circle. Although profitable, these part-swing machines were severely limited in their range. Operators wanted a wider cut with adequate room to load the coal and the capability to dump material anywhere within the machine's working radius. A fully revolving shovel was the obvious answer.

FIRST FULLY REVOLVING STRIPPING SHOVELS

The Bucyrus Company built the first full-circle long-boom stripping shovel in the United States soon after it purchased the Vulcan Steam Shovel Company in 1910. Known as the Class 5 and built to Vulcan designs, the fully revolving shovel carried a 1½–cubic yard (1.2–cubic meter) dipper on a 55-foot

Shovels with extra long booms, known as stripping shovels, were the preferred equipment to uncover relatively shallow coal seams in the fledgling surface mining industry of the early twentieth century. One of the first stripping shovels was this rail-mounted 150-B steam-powered machine, which appeared in 1911. With a 2 ½-yard dipper, it stripped coal near Pittsburg, Kansas.

As the surface coal mining industry matured, larger stripping shovels were needed. In 1914, Bucyrus responded with the 225-B. Weighing over 300 tons and wielding a 6-yard dipper on a 75-foot boom, this monster machine turned out to be the most popular stripping shovel ever produced. By 1923, over 90 had been placed in service.

(17-meter) boom. A total of three Class 5s were shipped to customers between 1910 and 1911, all working on coal stripping in the Pittsburg, Kansas, area. These machines worked well for their owners, attracting much attention from the industry and other manufacturers.

In 1911, Bucyrus' competitor, Marion, placed its first long-boom revolving stripping shovel in service near Danville, Illinois. The steam-powered, rail-mounted machine weighed 150 tons (136 tonnes) and carried a 3½–cubic yard (2.7–cubic meter) dipper. Its success prompted Bucyrus to quickly respond with two competitive machines, the 2½–cubic yard (1.9–cubic meter) 150-B and the 3½–cubic yard (2.7–cubic meter) 175-B stripping shovels. These rail-mounted steam machines featured an equalizing beam on one side of the undercarriage providing a three-point suspension system with screw jacks for leveling. By the end of 1912, one each of these two shovels was already put to work stripping coal in the southeast Kansas coal field.

SHOVEL SIZE INCREASES

Spurred on by the demands of World War I, the idea of stripping coal with large shovels caught on very quickly. During this period, the only two manufacturing companies in this business, Bucyrus and Marion, worked feverishly to introduce new models and capture the world record for size. In 1914, Bucyrus designed a new monster shovel for its day, the 225-B. It weighed over 300 tons (272 tonnes) and carried a 6-cubic yard (4.6–cubic meter) dipper on a 75-foot (23-meter) boom. By 1923, over 90 of these huge machines had been erected, making it the best-selling stripping shovel of all time.

Bucyrus helped pioneer the use of electricity as a power source for large stripping shovels. The company shipped its first electric stripper in 1917, but conventional electric motors at the time proved unsuitable for shovels because of their rapid cyclic power requirements. Two years later, Bucyrus first offered a new electrical-power system known as Ward–Leonard control

Another significant stripping shovel was the 320-B, launched in 1923. Carrying an 8-yard dipper and weighing 390 tons, it was the ultimate in steam shovels. With some sold as draglines, the 320-B was produced until 1930. Later versions were available with electric power and an optional 8-crawler undercarriage instead of the standard rail mounting.

Although Bucyrus had produced fully revolving excavators since 1912, there was still sufficient demand from customers preferring the traditional limited-swing railroad shovels to keep this type in production until the early 1930s. To extend their usefulness, Bucyrus offered crawler conversion kits to free the railroad shovel from its restrictive rails.

as an alternative to steam on its largest stripping shovel, the 225-B. The Ward-Leonard system, which became standard on all electric shovels up to the advent of the modern AC-driven machines, consisted of DC motors for each motion (hoist, drag, and swing) powered by DC generators driven by constant-speed AC (synchronous) electric motors. The Ward-Leonard system offered power characteristics similar to steam in that the DC motors' torque increased as their speed decreased, an appropriate solution to the cyclic nature of shovel loading.

In 1924, Bucyrus built its largest machine to date, the massive 320-B steam-powered stripping shovel, weighing 390 tons (354 tonnes) and carrying a dipper of 8 cubic yards (6.1 cubic meters). It was designed to compete with the Marion 350, a similar-sized shovel introduced a year earlier, and the 8–cubic yard (6.1–cubic meter) No. 300 made by Ruston & Hornsby Ltd. in England. At that time, these were the only three manufacturers in the world

building large shovels. The 320-B proved to be a great success, and 29 shovels plus 8 dragline versions were sold before the last one was shipped in 1930.

The steam versions of these three giant shovels of the 1920s, the Marion 350, the Bucyrus 320-B, and the Ruston No. 300, were the largest steam-powered shovels ever built. They were true marvels of the mechanical world and impressed all those who watched them. The unique hissing and snorting of the main hoisting engine, combined with the separate swing engines and the hissing of the crowd engine mounted on the boom must have created an unforgettable symphony, but was probably not appreciated by those working around the machine! As shovel dipper sizes continued to spiral above 8 cubic yards (6.1 cubic meters), all large excavators changed to relatively silent electric power.

In 1927, Bucyrus introduced the 750-B, forerunner of a long line of successful electric-powered stripping shovels. Ten of the 12–cubic yard

In 1927, Bucyrus introduced the 750-B, forerunner of a long line of successful giant stripping shovels. Early versions carried dippers of 12 cubic yards like the one shown here. It was located near Pittsburg, Kansas, and owned by the Pittsburg & Midway Coal Mining Company. After 1930, a new design with counterbalanced hoist raised the 750-B's capacity to 22 cubic yards.

The industry's first revolving shovel designed for heavy rock work in quarry and mines was the Bucyrus 120-B. It combined the ruggedness of the traditional railroad shovel with the flexibility of the revolving shovel. Available with steam or electric power, the 5-yard 120-B was a resounding success with over 300 built up to 1951.

(9–cubic meter) 750-Bs were delivered up to 1930. The Michigan Limestone Company of Rogers City, Michigan, then asked Bucyrus-Erie Company if they could design a more efficient 750-B. The result was the first shovel to be fitted with a counterbalanced hoist system, increasing the 750-B's capacity nearly 50 percent to 18 cubic yards (14 cubic meters) and, more importantly, using less power. The first of this new breed was delivered to Michigan Limestone in 1930.

The counterbalanced hoist consisted of a moving counterweight located at the rear of the revolving frame and connected to the dipper hoist drum through its own set of wire ropes. The counterweight ran vertically in a cage similar to an elevator, balancing the weight of the empty dipper. Thus, all the

hoisting power could be applied to filling the dipper and hoisting the load. Three more 750-Bs with the counterbalance hoist system were delivered, the last in 1940. These included a second machine for the Michigan Limestone Company, though by that time its capacity had increased to 22 cubic yards (17 cubic meters).

INDUSTRY'S FIRST QUARRY AND MINE SHOVELS

In the 1920s, quarries and hard-rock mines were expanding their use of shovels to load haulage vehicles. The most common vehicles at that time were railcars, and the only shovels heavy and robust enough for quarry work were the old faithful steam railroad shovels. However, these could not swing 360

The success of the 120-B quarry and mine shovel prompted Bucyrus to add similarly-designed models to its range. By 1929, the mining shovel line was extended downward to the 2 ¼-yard 75-B and upward to the 6 ½-yard 170-B. Included was this 3 ½-yard steam powered 100-B.

The largest of the early quarry and mine shovels was the 170-B introduced in 1929. Weighing some 245 tons, it was a favorite in the Iron Ranges around Hibbing, Minnesota, and the anthracite region of eastern Pennsylvania. This one is owned by A.E. Dick Construction Company and is uncovering rich anthracite at Locust Gap, Pennsylvania.

degrees, a distinct disadvantage for loading haulage vehicles, and their need for rail tracks made them awkward and time consuming to move. The only shovels able to swing 360 degrees were small construction-sized shovels or long-boomed gangly stripping shovels, which were not robust enough for hard digging. This situation led Bucyrus to design a shovel that combined the railroad shovel's robustness with the stripping shovel's full-swing capability.

The 120-B was introduced as the world's first fully rotating electric mine and quarry shovel designed for loading rail cars or trucks. First built in 1925 as a 4-cubic yard (3.1–cubic meter) machine, it was soon upped to 5–cubic yard (3.8–cubic meter) capacity and revolutionized the shovel industry, selling over 300 around the world until 1951. The 120-B was the forerunner of a long line of Bucyrus electric quarry and mine shovels. It was soon joined by the similarly-designed 3 ½-cubic yard (2.7–cubic meter) 100-B (1926); the 2 ¼-cubic yard (1.7–cubic meter) 75-B (1928); the 6 ½-cubic yard (5–cubic meter) 170-B (1929); and the 3 ¼-cubic yard (2.5–cubic meter) 85-B (1935). With the exception of the 75-B, all remained in the line until the early 1950s.

INNOVATIVE STRIPPING SHOVELS

In 1935, Bucyrus-Erie captured the title of manufacturer of the world's largest machine when it introduced the innovative 950-B stripping shovel. The first one was shipped to Shasta Coal Company in Bicknell, Indiana. This 30–cubic yard (23–cubic meter) stripper featured the counterbalanced hoist system introduced on the earlier 750-B, but it also included many innovations that have remained in the Bucyrus shovel design ever since. The front end arrangement, with a single tubular dipper handle operated by wire ropes, was the most notable feature. The handle's tubular design allowed it to rotate, thereby minimizing stresses on the handle and boom caused by unbalanced loads on the dipper. The rope-operated crowd motion (handle extension and retraction) allowed the crowd machinery and motor to be mounted on the revolving frame where it minimized swing inertia and saved energy. The two-part boom was pinned at its center and tied back to the gantry with two beams, eliminating bending stresses at the boom center and permitting a boom of much lighter construction.

One of the most popular shovels in the 1920s was the 50-B. Launched by Bucyrus in 1922, this 2-yard shovel was available with steam, gasoline, diesel, and electric power and convertible to shovel, dragline, and crane. It was equally at home on construction sites or loading ore into trucks in surface mines.

When the innovative Bucyrus-Erie 950-B stripping shovel went to work in 1935, it was the world's largest shovel. The larger 1050-B appeared in 1941 with standard 33-yard dipper and operating weight of 1,500 tons. Both machines pioneered many features that have remained in Bucyrus shovel designs ever since, such as the tubular handle, rope crowd, and lower works propel.

Marion introduced the knee-action crowd on a 35-yard model 5561 in 1941. It improved the performance and range of large stripping shovels by pivoting the dipper handle to a moveable stiff leg instead of attaching it to the shipper shaft. All subsequent Marion and two Bucyrus-Erie stripping shovels adopted this design.

The lower works of the 950-B did not escape radical improvements either. A propelling motor was mounted in each of the four crawler assemblies, eliminating the previous complicated system of multiple gear trains, shafts, and jaw clutches. For the first time on a Bucyrus-Erie machine, a hydraulic leveling system was introduced, dispensing with the earlier screw types. This system automatically leveled the machine utilizing a pendulum device to control the oil in the four support cylinders. Steering was effected through large horizontal hydraulic cylinders acting on the crawler assemblies. The 950-B had an operating weight of nearly 1,250 tons (1,134 tonnes).

Bucyrus-Erie shipped ten 950-B shovels until 1941, when it upgraded it to the similarly designed 1050-B, with increased capacity to 33 cubic yards (25 cubic meters). This was in response to Marion's 1940 introduction of an innovative stripping shovel, the 35–cubic yard (27–cubic meter) model 5561, featuring knee-action crowd. Knee-action crowd was a radical new design of front-end geometry for stripping shovels where the dipper handle was attached to a stiff leg pivoting at the boom foot, instead of the handle attached

Beginning in 1950, Bucyrus-Erie redesigned its successful quarry and mine machine line, which had been a big money maker for the company and its customers. The 100-B was replaced by the 4 ½-yard 110-B. The 110-B incorporated many of the successful features found on the large stripping shovels.

In 1952, the successful 170-B quarry and mine shovel was upgraded to the 9-yard 190-B. This larger shovel complimented the already released 110-B and 150-B models, further contributing to Bucyrus-Erie as a leader in hard rock mining equipment. This powerful threesome remained in production for over 25 years.

to the mid-point of the boom. The moveable stiff leg allowed the dipper to move in a long horizontal sweep at ground level, resulting in a long clean-up radius with the dipper teeth less likely to gouge into the coal being uncovered. Its other advantages include reduced swing inertia due to the crowd machinery mounted near the machine's center of rotation and reduced bending stresses in the boom. The knee-action crowd became standard for all subsequent Marion stripping shovels, and later, some Bucyrus shovels.

Meanwhile, Bucyrus–Erie continued to improve upon its successful 1050–B, gradually increasing the capacity to 45 cubic yards (34 cubic meters). Shipments included two to Old Ben Coal Company of Indiana and Peabody Coal Company, who eventually owned five of the twelve 1050-Bs built. The last was delivered in 1960 to United Electric Coal Company's Banner Mine in Illinois. This machine operated until 2003, latterly at the company's Industry Mine in Illinois, the company having changed its name to Freeman–United Coal Mining Company.

Customers' demands for lower unit costs by the use of larger equipment spawned the 280-B, unveiled in 1962. The new larger mining shovel with 15 cubic yards of nominal capacity proved an economic match for any off-highway truck available at that time. A special long-range version with 8-yard dipper is shown working in a chalk quarry in England.

In the 60–cubic yard class, the 1650-B stripping shovel was Bucyrus-Erie's response to Marion's famous Mountaineer shovel of similar capacity. Launched in 1956, it helped to satisfy the need of America's Midwest coal companies, who demanded larger machines to uncover deeper coal reserves in one pass.

MINING SHOVELS IMPROVED

Beginning in 1950, with over 650 of its electric mining shovels (models 75–B to 170–B) already delivered to satisfied customers, Bucyrus-Erie superseded its machines with a new line of totally redesigned models. The company was following through with its belief that technology never stands still. New manufacturing techniques, improved materials, and a continual stream of innovative designs evolved to improve productivity and lower operating costs. The new shovel design was really a result of experience gained from the company's successful stripping shovels, as several features found on the larger machines were included. Of these, the most notable were the single tubular dipper handle with rope crowd, which replaced the former twin stick rack-and-pinion design, and the two–part boom that eliminated bending stresses.

The three shovels that opened the door to a new era in Bucyrus-Erie's mining shovel design included the 4 ½–cubic yard (3.4–cubic meter) 110-B, the 6–cubic yard (4.6–cubic meter) 150-B, and 9–cubic yard (6.9–cubic meter) 190-B. These modern machines immediately replaced their former counterparts and became the foundation of all subsequent Bucyrus mining shovels.

In the early 1960s, the big open pit mines producing iron ore, copper, and anthracite were expanding. They were looking for a mining shovel bigger than the current top-of-the-line 9–cubic yard (6.9–cubic meter) 190-B. Bucyrus-Erie responded with the 280-B, a modern shovel with dippers ranging from 8 to 18 cubic yards (6 to 14 cubic meters), depending on the intended material. The first 280-B went to work in 1962 at Kaiser Steel's Eagle Mountain iron ore mine in California, and by year end, seven of the new shovels had been shipped to iron and coal mines in Canada and the United States. The 280-B was well-proven when it went to work, as it was actually an upgrade from the lighter 270-B, a 12–cubic yard (9–cubic meter) shovel of similar capacity introduced two years earlier. Five of these shovels were already at work, including two long-boom 8–cubic yard (6.1–cubic meter) versions in the Kentucky coal mines of Peabody Coal Company and Green Coal Company. The 270-B was the first shovel to be equipped with static control, utilizing solid state components in place of rotating units, which provided instantaneous response and greater digging forces. The 280-B successfully followed in its footsteps, with 95 being sold up to 1982.

The 1960s was the decade of gigantic stripping machines, the size of which has never been exceeded. Here is Bucyrus-Erie's largest-ever shovel, the 3850-B with 140-yard dipper. Commencing work in 1964, it swung a boom 200 feet long, weighs 9,350 tons, with each of its eight crawler assemblies measuring 40 feet long.

This close-up shows the massive proportions of the 140–cubic yard dipper and sheave arrangement of the 3850-B. The machine was accessed by an elevator running up the center of the machine. Peabody Coal Company operated this giant at its River King Mine in Illinois.

THE GIANT STRIPPING SHOVELS

In the 1950s, coal companies began to face increasing depths of overburden as most of the shallow coal was being worked out. This, coupled with the increasing demand for coal, produced a demand for even larger, more efficient stripping machines. The Hanna Coal Company (now Consolidation Coal Company) ordered a shovel of unbelievable proportions for their operations in eastern Ohio. Much larger than anything before, the Mountaineer took its first bite in January 1956, and the era of giant stripping shovels was born. The Marion-built monster, type 5760, wielded a 60–cubic yard (46–cubic meter) dipper and could tackle a face over 100 feet (30 meters) high. Almost immediately, Bucyrus-Erie responded with a shovel of similar size, the 55–cubic yard (42–cubic meter) 1650-B River Queen ordered by Peabody Coal Company for their River Queen Mine in Kentucky. Both Bucyrus-Erie and Marion placed several more large stripping shovels in this size range in service before the end of the decade.

Another big stripping shovel was this 1850-B owned by the Pittsburg & Midway Coal Mining Company in Kansas. Commissioned in 1963, it carried a 90-yard dipper, stood 150 feet tall and was equipped with a 150-foot boom. This machine is now preserved at the Big Brutus Historical Landmark near West Mineral, Kansas.

In 1960, Bucyrus-Erie secured an order for the world's largest shovel, a model 3850-B with a dipper capacity of 115 cubic yards (88 cubic meters)—almost double the size of largest shovel then in operation! Christened the Big Hog, it went to work in 1962 at Peabody Coal Company's Sinclair Mine in Kentucky. As with all large stripping shovels, the 3850-B was supported on four two-crawler propelling assemblies, each carrying a 54-inch (137-centimeter) diameter hydraulic cylinder to support and level the machine. Each crawler

This picture taken in 2003 shows the Silver Spade, one of two 1950-B stripping shovels sold to Consolidation Coal Company (Consol) for coal mining in southeast Ohio. Starting work in 1965, the Silver Spade is one of the last remaining stripping shovels in operation. The 7,200-ton machine is equipped with knee-action crowd and wields a 105–cubic yard dipper. *Photo used by permission of CONSOL Energy, Inc.*

The 150-RB, the Ruston-Bucyrus version of the 150-B made in Lincoln, England, was a favorite of British opencast coal mining contractors in the 1960s. The 6-yard shovel was the perfect match for the 45-ton standard-size trucks in use at that time. Large numbers of the 150-RB were also exported to Africa, South America, and many European countries.

Another popular mining shovel made in Lincoln, England, was the 195-B. From 1974 to 1985, 44 of these 13-yard shovels were produced, most of which found their way into British surface coal mines. A significant number were also exported to countries such India, Brazil, Spain, and Egypt.

The 21-yard 295-B shovel was introduced in 1972, just in time to satiate the rapid increasing demands for coal in the 1970s. Many were shipped to Wyoming where the 295-B was found ideal to uncover and load the thick coal seams of low-sulfur coal found under relatively shallow overburden.

measured 40 feet (12 meters) long by 8 feet (2.4 meters) high and carried 37 shoes, each 7 feet 6 inches (2.3 meters) wide and weighing almost 2 tons (1.8 tonnes). It took 300 railcars to transport all components from the South Milwaukee manufacturing facility to the Kentucky mine site. The working weight of the entire machine was estimated at 9,000 tons (8,165 tonnes).

Before the first 3850-B was commissioned, Bucyrus-Erie received an order from Peabody Coal Company for a second 3850-B shovel. This machine, with a slightly different boom configuration, carried a 140–cubic yard (107–cubic meter) dipper and weighed nearly 9,350 tons (8,482 tonnes). It began digging in 1964 at the River King Mine in Illinois, and was the largest shovel ever built by Bucyrus-Erie.

The race for the largest stripping shovel ended in 1965, when Marion Power Shovel broke the final record for shovel size, a record that still stands today. The incredible Marion 6360, named The Captain, was purchased by the Southwestern Illinois Coal Corporation to work at its Captain Mine near Percy, Illinois. The shovel boom measured 215 feet (66 meters) long, and the

dipper held 180 cubic yards (138 cubic meters). With an estimated operating weight of 15,000 tons (13,600 tonnes) after additional modifications, this behemoth was truly the captain of all shovels, as it was the largest machine of any type to move under its own power on land.

Bucyrus-Erie's final stripping shovels were the two 1950-Bs purchased by the Hanna Coal Company (now Consolidation Coal Company) for coal stripping in southeastern Ohio. The first, named The Silver Spade, started work in 1965, swinging a 105-cubic yard (81–cubic meter) dipper on a 200-foot (61-meter) boom. The second, The Gem of Egypt, went to work two years later with a shorter, 170-foot (52-meter) boom but with a 130–cubic yard (99–cubic meter) dipper. They weighed 7,200 tons (6,532 tonnes) and 6,850 tons (6,214 tonnes), respectively. The Gem was scrapped in 1992 because of diminishing coal reserves, but the older Silver Spade continues to uncover coal to help satisfy the nation's demand for electric power.

The largest stripping shovel ever built, and the heaviest machine ever to move on land, was the Marion 6360 stripping shovel known as "The Captain." With its 15,000-ton operating weight and 180–cubic yard bucket, this behemoth amazed even hardened surface miners used to working with monster machines. Its life came to an abrupt end in 1991 when The Captain had to be scrapped following a disastrous fire.

Bucyrus-Erie achieved a major breakthrough in mining shovel technology in 1979, when it introduced the 34-yard 395-B. The new shovel was the first to incorporate variable-frequency AC electric motors and controls called Acutrol, replacing the traditional DC Ward-Leonard system that had been in use since the 1920s.

LARGER MINING SHOVELS

As mentioned in Chapter 1, the Arab Oil Embargo of the early 1970s generated an unprecedented demand for surface mining equipment. Most of the company's machine orders were for draglines, but shovels received their fair share of attention. To cope with this increased demand, Bucyrus-Erie unveiled a larger mining shovel in 1972 in the 21–cubic yard (16–cubic meter) class. The new 295-B succeeded the 280-B but included more advanced features by utilizing the latest technology. It was found to be the perfect size for new coal mines opening up in the Powder River Basin, Wyoming, where the initial overburden was shallow and could be removed efficiently with truck and shovel fleets. The same fleets could also excavate and haul the coal. The 295-B soon became the standard shovel size in America's large surface coal mines and was an excellent match for the 170-ton

When Bucyrus acquired Marion Power Shovel in 1997, some of the former Marion machines were kept in the Bucyrus product line. The popular 182M with dipper range from 10 to 23 cubic yards is still sold to the Indian surface coal mining industry.

(154-tonne) haul trucks, the standard size of the day. More than 100 295-B's went to work over a 12-year period.

In 1979, Bucyrus-Erie announced the 395-B, a major breakthrough in mining shovel technology. The new, larger shovel was the first to incorporate variable-frequency AC electric motors and controls called Acutrol. This system replaced the former DC motors and rotating motor-generator sets of the Ward-Leonard control system, which had been the norm in electric excavators since the 1920s. The first 395-B, with a 34–cubic yard (26–cubic meter) dipper, was shipped to Anamax at their Twin Buttes copper mine in Arizona. This pioneering shovel offered new levels of productivity with its fast electrical response and lower power consumption, and signaled the direction of future mining shovel technology.

Another jump in shovel size occurred in 1990 with the introduction of the 495-B. This new model was designed on similar lines to the 395-B but with more power and further advanced electrical features allowing it to carry a 53–cubic yard (41–cubic meter) dipper.

MARION SHOVELS ADDED

In 1997, when Bucyrus took over the Marion Power Shovel Company, it gained access to all of Marion's designs, patents, and technology. Customers could now select the "best of both worlds" from the two lines of mining equipment. Marion's shovel history had followed closely to that of Bucyrus with several notable achievements to its credit, including the world's largest stripping shovel and knee-action crowd. Marion and Bucyrus had been arch

Marion's flagship mining shovel at the time of the 1997 takeover was the 351M with nominal capacity of 57 cubic yards. The well-proven machine at the cutting edge of technology had evolved from the former 301M of the mid 1980s. It was continued by Bucyrus as the 595B.

The first High Performance 495HF was delivered in 2002 to Albian Sands Energy Inc. for work in Alberta oilsands operations. The HF (High Flotation) version is equipped with 140-inch wide crawler shoes to combat the soft underfoot conditions. Four more 495HF shovels have since been delivered to the same site.

rivals in the stripping shovel field as each vied for the "largest stripping shovel" title from the early days through the 1960s. In 1951, Marion shipped the first 10–cubic yard (7.7–cubic meter) 191M mining shovel, the largest on two crawlers at that time. This model proved to be one of Marion's most popular shovels with 156 sold up to 1989, by which time its capacity had

been upped to 15 cubic yards (12 cubic meters). The Marion 15–cubic yard (12–cubic meter) 291M long range shovel took over the title for the largest on two crawlers when two were shipped to Peabody Coal Company in 1963.

Certain former Marion models were retained in Bucyrus' expanded line because of their popularity and advanced design features. These included Marion's 182M, which had experienced steady sales from its introduction in 1966. In fact, a 182M was the last machine shipped from the Marion, Ohio, plant. Marion's flagship mining shovel, the 351M in the 57–cubic yard (44–cubic meter) class, with certain upgrades, was renumbered the Bucyrus 595B. This machine was an outgrowth of the former 301M, which Marion had introduced in 1986. Suncor Energy currently operates the entire gamut of these models, from the 301M to the latest 595B, at their oilsands open pit mines in Alberta, Canada.

The 495HR is the Hard Rock version in the 495 series of mining shovels. It combines the heavy-duty undercarriage from the former Marion 351M design with upper works featuring the latest technology in AC electrical variable frequency control. This one works in Nevada at the Robinson Mine of Quadra Mining Ltd.

CHAPTER
THREE

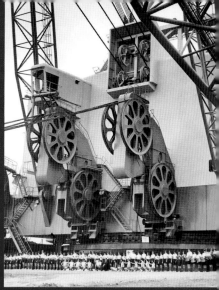

DRAGLINES

THE FIRST DRAGLINES

In 1910, Bucyrus entered the dragline market after purchasing manufacturing rights for the Heyworth-Newman dragline excavator. A number of these machines had been operating successfully by James O. Heyworth, one of several drainage contractors working in the Chicago area who had developed their own machines. Based on the Heyworth patents, Bucyrus developed the Class series of specialized dragline machines starting in 1911 with the Class 24, the world's largest at the time carrying a 3 ½–cubic yard (2.7–cubic meter) bucket on a 100-foot (30-meter) boom.

Bucyrus sold over 370 of the Class series machines, but none of these were walking draglines. They were mounted on rails, skids and rollers, or crawler tracks. While these worked profitably for their owners, Bucyrus management noted the rising success of a competitive dragline manufacturer whose machines were equipped with a patented walking device. This was the Monighan Machine Company of Chicago, who had built non-walking draglines in collaboration with Page prior to 1912 and then became an independent dragline builder. Oscar Martinson, a young engineer with Monighan, had observed the restrictions and labor-intensive methods of moving the rail- and skid-mounted draglines and the high ground pressure

Opposite: Bucyrus entered the dragline business after purchasing manufacturing rights for the Heyworth-Newman dragline excavator in 1910. From this early design, Bucyrus developed the Class-series draglines, such as this steam-powered Class 24, the largest in its day with 3 ½-yard bucket on a 100-foot boom.

Early draglines were not
equipped with any means of
propel drive. They were mounted
on skids and rollers and dragged
themselves along using their
bucket. This view showing the
arrangement of the heavy
skids, hardwood rollers, and
timber tracking illustrates this
cumbersome method of moving
a large machine.

exerted by the crawler types. So he invented a walking device by attaching two moveable shoes, one on each side of the dragline's revolving frame. This brainwave changed dragline mobility forever. The first walking device was known as the Martinson Tractor and was fitted to Monighan 1-T and 3-T (1–cubic yard and 3–cubic yard [2.3–cubic meter]) draglines in 1913. By 1924, the line had been broadened to seven T-series models up to the 4-T at 4–cubic yard (3.1–cubic meter) capacity.

BUCYRUS-MONIGHAN WALKING DRAGLINES

The simplicity of Monighan's walking system was the key to its success. Each shoe was suspended by chains from a beam, which in turn was hung from an eccentric trunnion. A propel shaft running across the entire width of the revolving frame rotated the trunnions and shoes in a circular motion so that both shoes touched the ground at the same time and lifted the rear of the machine off the ground. As the propel shaft continued to turn, the machine

pulled itself backwards a distance of one step and then lowered itself gently back to the ground. The shoes continued to rotate, and the process was repeated step by step. When digging, the dragline sat on its circular base or tub and the shoes hung from the revolving frame at the side of the machine. In 1925, Martinson improved his patented walking system by changing the chains to a cam wheel running in an oval track in a frame pivoted to the shoes. The new W-series machines went into production, starting with the first 3-W in 1925, and immediately rendered the existing T-series machines obsolete.

With the new walking system successfully established, Monighan built several record-beating draglines. The 6–cubic yard (4.6–cubic meter) 6-W appeared in 1926 with a standard 100-foot (31-meter) boom, followed by the

The Class 14 dragline was the first Bucyrus machine of any type to be equipped with crawler tracks. Appearing in 1912, the first tracks consisted of hardwood shoes mounted on a primitive chain arrangement. The picture shows a later diesel-electric Class 14 dragline excavating drainage ditches in Iowa.

Before walking draglines became universally employed in surface mines, some large crawler draglines were built throughout the 1920s. This Class 375 of 1929 stripped phosphate in Florida. The massive electric-powered machine boasted an 8-crawler undercarriage and could carry buckets with up to 10 cubic yards capacity.

6150 in 1929 with a 150-foot (46-meter) boom. The 10–cubic yard (7.7–cubic meter) threshold was reached in 1934 with the launch of the 10-W. Most of these Monighans were sold as diesel machines with the drums operated through clutches and brakes. Nearly all were equipped with Fairbanks-Morse or Cooper-Bessemer slow-revving marine-type engines (350 to 450 rpm). The four-digit model series (6150, 6160, and 8160) denoted the standard bucket size and boom length; e.g. the 8160 swung an 8-cubic yard (6.1-cubic meter) bucket on a 160-foot (49-meter) boom.

Bucyrus-Erie Company purchased an interest in the Monighan company in 1931 and changed its name to the Bucyrus-Monighan Company after taking full control in 1934. The former Monighan plant in Chicago was retained. This gave Bucyrus-Erie access to all the walking dragline designs, with immediate results. In 1935, Bucyrus-Erie unveiled the 950-B, the largest dragline built up to that time. It swung a 12–cubic yard (9–cubic meter) bucket

A walking system was the answer to a dragline's poor maneuverability. In 1913, Oscar Martinson of the Monighan Machine Company of Chicago invented a walking device consisting of two shoes suspended by chains on each side of the machine. This simple device is shown on a small model 1-T of one cubic yard capacity.

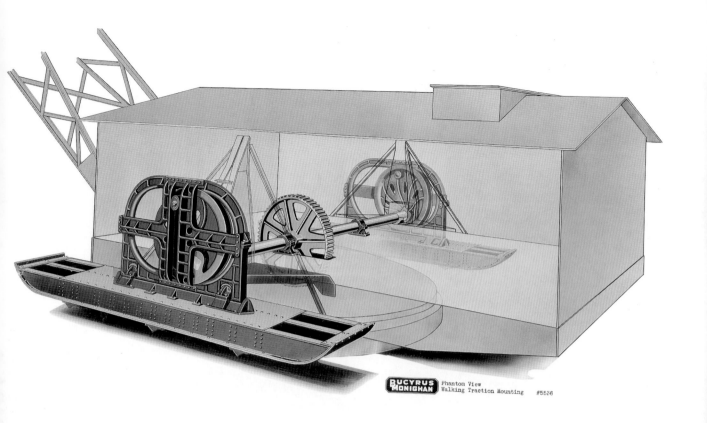

In 1925, Martinson improved his dragline walking system to a more positive arrangement that consisted of an eccentric wheel running in an oval roller path. This method retained its simplicity with a single walk shaft running across the width of the machine as shown in the ghost illustration. Bucyrus-Erie formed the Bucyrus-Monighan Company in 1934.

on a 250-foot (76-meter) boom, the longest in the world, and its operating weight was just over 1,000 tons (907 tonnes). This machine was shipped to the Lone Star Cement Company in Brazil, where it was used to strip limestone in a large quarry. The 950-B was regarded as an engineering masterpiece and laid the foundation for much larger Bucyrus-Erie machines, which appeared over the next three decades.

The Martinson walking system was considered unbeatable for small and medium walking draglines. The single drive shaft and shoes are all that are required for propel. There are no complicated drive trains or motors in the dragline's base or tub, and the large diameter of the tub reduces ground pressure to a minimum. To Martinson's credit, his walking system was retained when Bucyrus-Erie took over Monighan and has remained current on Bucyrus machines right up to the present day for machines up to 70–cubic yard (54–cubic meter) capacity.

One of the most successful small walking draglines was the Bucyrus-Monighan 5-W, designed and built in the Chicago plant. Released in 1935 as a 5–cubic yard (3.8–cubic meter) dragline carrying a 120-foot (37-meter)

One of the first draglines to sport Monighan's revised propel system was the 6-W, launched in 1926. Shown here on a coal stripping job, the 6-W could carry a 6-yard bucket on a 120-foot boom. Electric or diesel power was available for Bucyrus-Monighan machines. Low ground pressure and long reach were their main attributes.

For some unknown reason, Monighan designated a number of machines with a model number different from the normal W series. This model 6160 indicated it carried a 6-yard bucket on a 160-foot boom. Monighan installed low-speed diesel engines in its draglines, sometimes as low as 450 rpm, supplied by such firms as Fairbanks-Morse and Cooper-Bessemer.

boom, it was available with either diesel or electric power. The 5-W was popular in surface mines, gravel pits, irrigation projects, and all types of construction work. It still holds the all-time best-selling record for a walking dragline. A total of 79 of these popular draglines were built in the Chicago plant, and a further 62 were built in the Ruston-Bucyrus plant at Lincoln, England, over a production life that lasted until 1971. One is preserved in a surface mining interpretive center at Estevan, Saskatchewan, Canada.

Just prior to World War II, the very popular 7-W and 9-W machines were added to the range. After the war, other new machines were introduced, including the first 200-W (6 cubic yards [4.6 cubic meters]) in 1945 and the 500-W (12 cubic yards [9 cubic meters]) in 1946. These machines, along with

In 1935, Bucyrus-Erie shipped the world's largest dragline to a limestone quarry in Brazil. The 950-B weighed 1,000 tons and swung a 12-yard bucket on a 250-foot boom, the world's longest. It proved the Monighan walking system would work well on large machines and paved the way for even larger machines.

The 5-W, offering diesel or electric power, was designed and built in the Chicago plant of Bucyrus-Monighan. Popular in small- and medium-sized stripping operations, the handy 5-yard walker still holds the all-time best-selling record for a walking dragline. The Chicago plant shipped 79, while another 62 were built in the British plant at Lincoln.

the big diesel-powered 450-W and the 480-W (14 cubic yards [11 cubic meters]), kept the Chicago plant busy until its closure in 1958. The diesel-powered Bucyrus-Monighan draglines were usually specified with either Cooper-Bessemer or Fairbanks-Morse engines running at a slow 450 rpm and producing up to 1,000 horsepower (746 kilowatts) in the case of the 480-W. The last machine shipped from the Chicago plant was a 7-W early in 1958, before walking dragline manufacture was transferred to South Milwaukee.

Another milestone machine was the Bucyrus-Erie 1150-B, built at South Milwaukee and launched in 1944. Developed from the 950-B walker, which had appeared almost a decade earlier, the 1150-B carried buckets in the range from 20 to 25 cubic yards (15 to 19 cubic meters) and weighed approximately 1,200 tons (1,089 tonnes). Its circular tub measured 44 feet (13 meters) in diameter, and the machine was offered with booms from 180 to 215 feet (55 to 66 meters) long.

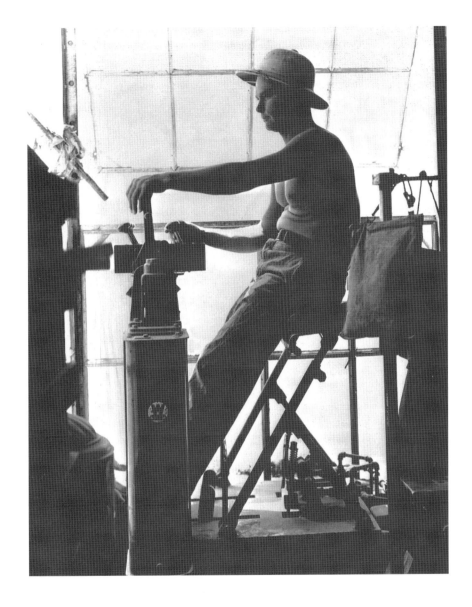

Prior to the 1950s, operator comfort was not factored into the design of excavators. This operator controls a 5-W walking dragline. His left hand is on the electric rheostat controller for the swing motion, while his right hand throws the switches for the air-controlled clutches. He has two foot pedals for the air-controlled brakes.

Sixteen 1150-Bs were delivered in the United States prior to 1950. However, after only a few years' work, four of these were dismantled and shipped to the United Kingdom under the Lend-Lease Program following World War II. There, the machines assisted with the rapid recovery of much-needed coal. All four machines had a long working life in their new home, operating well into the 1980s. One machine is now preserved by a private preservation society, the St. Aidans Trust, at a mining interpretive site near Leeds, Yorkshire. In 1950, the seventeenth and last new 1150-B also went to the United Kingdom to strip overburden from iron ore deposits at Corby, Northamptonshire, where it worked until 1980.

Bucyrus-Erie launched the 1150-B in 1944, the largest built to that time by the company. The 1,200-ton machine swung buckets from 20 to 25 cubic yards on booms to 215 feet. Of the 16 built, 5 were shipped to the United Kingdom to assist with coal and iron ore recovery following World War II. One of these is currently preserved near Leeds, England. This one is shown stripping overburden and loading it into a hopper at a northern Minnesota iron mine.

DRAGLINE SIZE INCREASES

In 1951, Bucyrus-Erie upgraded the 1150-B to the 1250-B, a dragline with more power and capacity than its forerunner. Power was increased to 500 horsepower (373 kilowatts) for its two hoist and two drag motors, and 150 horsepower (112 kilowatts) for its three swing motors. Booms up to 235 feet (72 meters) and buckets up to 33 cubic yards (25 cubic meters) were offered. After shipping eight 1250-Bs, Bucyrus-Erie upgraded its largest dragline again in 1959 and designated it the 1250-W. Besides a modest increase in capacity to 35 cubic yards (27 cubic meters) and longer booms up to 245 feet (75 meters), the 1250-W's most distinguishing feature was its radical two-part boom design. The upper part of the boom was suspended by ropes from a mast pivoted on the lower section. The idea was to facilitate changing boom lengths by adding different-length top sections. Of the six 1250-W's built, four were shipped to the phosphate fields of Florida, while the other two stripped coal in Pennsylvania. One of these joined its brothers in Florida in 2003.

Rounding out the 1200-series draglines was the modern looking 1260-W, which first appeared in 1965. With buckets ranging from 30 to 42 cubic yards (23 to 32 cubic meters), this dragline sported a computer-designed triangular boom with tubular members. It had three main chord members instead of the usual four. The 1260-W turned out to be one of Bucyrus-Erie's most popular draglines, with 33 being sold up to 1990. The last one went to work in 1992 for NB Coal Ltd. in New Brunswick, Canada. This machine moved south for a second life in Florida in 2000.

In 1963, the next jump in size occurred when Bucyrus-Erie shipped its first 60–cubic yard (46–cubic meter) 1450-W dragline to Pittsburg & Midway Coal Mining Company's Colonial Mine in Kentucky. This top-of-the-line machine did not hold its title long; the following year, Bucyrus-Erie shipped the first 2550-W to one of Ayrshire Collieries (AMAX) Company's mines in Indiana. The same company purchased the second of this model a year later, while two more were shipped to Texas Gulf Sulphur in North Carolina, and Pittsburg & Midway's Colonial Mine. The 75–cubic yard

The operator of this Bucyrus-Erie 1150-B commands a panoramic view of his work from the high-positioned cab. The operator needs only two hand levers—one for hoist and one for drag motions—and two foot pedals for swing to control this giant excavator. The fairleads for the twin drag ropes and boom foot pins can be seen.

Another small walker, the 200-W was unveiled in 1945. With a 5- or 6-yard bucket, it found favor with sand and gravel operations, quarries, and small to medium surface mines. Of the 55 built, many were shipped overseas to countries such as Thailand, Australia, Sweden, Finland, France, and England.

(57–cubic meter) 2550-Ws were equipped with booms 275 or 300 feet (84 or 91 meters) long and featured a new walking system known as the cam and slide system. Designed by Bucyrus-Erie for machines greater than 70–cubic yard (54–cubic meter) capacity, it featured an eccentric wheel running in a roller bearing and a greased shoe-mounted rail on which the machine moved through the action of the eccentric.

BIG MUSKIE

A proud moment in Bucyrus-Erie's history was achieved when Big Muskie, model 4250-W walking dragline, began to uncover coal at the Central Ohio Coal Company's Muskingum Mine near Cumberland, Ohio, in 1969. One

of the engineering marvels of the twentieth century, this machine still holds the title of largest dragline ever built. Swinging a bucket of 220 cubic yards (168 cubic meters) on a 310-foot (94-meter) boom and weighing some 14,500 tons (13,154 tonnes), the dragline exceeded the previous world's largest by over 50 percent. The previous largest was the Marion 8900 at 145 cubic yards (111 cubic meters), which had gone to work a couple of years earlier.

Big Muskie measured 487 feet (148 meters) long including the boom, and 151 feet (46 meters) wide. That's the length of a football field and wider than an 8-lane divided highway. The 220–cubic yard (168–cubic meter) bucket could hold an average two-story house. It took 340 railcars and 260 truckloads to ship the thousands of components to the site, where it took two years to erect. The 220–cubic yard (168–cubic meter) bucket, weighing 550

Distinguished by its unique two-part boom, the Bucyrus-Erie 1250-W swung the world's largest dragline bucket in 1960. The two-part boom idea facilitated rapid changes in boom length. The machine shown is one of five to work in the Florida phosphate fields with its 35-yard bucket and 225-foot boom.

The 1260-W turned out to be one of Bucyrus-Erie's most popular large draglines with 33 shipped from 1965 to 1992. It handled buckets from 30 to 40 cubic yards, depending on boom length. The one shown was the first made; it was shipped to Reynolds Mining Corporation at Bauxite, Arkansas, in 1965.

tons (499 tonnes) with load, was suspended by four wire hoist ropes and four drag ropes, all 5 inches (13 centimeters) in diameter—the biggest ropes ever manufactured at that time.

Inside the house, ten 1,000-horsepower (746 kilowatt) DC electric motors powered twin 11-foot (3.4-meter) diameter hoist drums through pinions and bull gears. A similar system powered the drag motion, utilizing eight 1,000-horsepower (746-kilowatt) motors. Another ten 625-horsepower (466-kilowatt) motors powered the swing motion through separate gear reductions and pinions, which meshed with the 75-foot (23-meter) diameter swing gear. To propel, Big Muskie used a unique walking system consisting of four hydraulically-powered shoes with two pinned together on each side. The shoes were raised and lowered by vertical hydraulic rams, which lifted the base of the machine entirely off the ground, unlike the usual method where the rear of the circular base trails on the ground. A further four horizontal

hydraulic rams, two on each side, pushed the machine through a 14-foot (4.3-meter) step while in the raised position.

After a useful life at Muskingum, Big Muskie was shut down in 1991 and scrapped in 1999. As an epitaph to one of the world's greatest engineering feats, one of the 220–cubic yard (168–cubic meter) buckets has been saved. It now rests in a public park not far from where Big Muskie made the earth move.

BIG DRAGLINES FOR THE COAL BOOM

The Arab Oil Embargo of the early 1970s created an increase in the need for large draglines. Coal production was seen as the answer to the United States' energy crisis. Traditional coal companies expanded their production, but others, such as oil companies new to the business, purchased coal properties. They all clamored to place orders for draglines. Bucyrus-Erie and other dragline

In the 1960s, the size of draglines escalated in leaps and bounds. The old faithful Monighan walking system served machines well up to 70 yards capacity, but a different system was required to propel the new breed of machines weighing over 4,000 tons. Ayrshire Collieries purchased the first two 75-yard 2550-Ws in 1964, the first to utilize the cam-and-slide walking system.

Bucyrus is proud to have built one of the engineering marvels of the twentieth century. The 4250-W walking dragline, named Big Muskie, went to work for the Central Ohio Coal Company in 1969. Swinging a 220-yard bucket on a 310-foot boom and weighing some 14,400 tons, the dragline exceeded the previous world's largest by over 50 percent.

manufacturers placed large numbers of new draglines in operation. However, none ever equaled the size of Big Muskie. Mine operators preferred slightly smaller models, designed with new technology but based on proven principles. They proved more reliable and, in some cases, actually out-produced the much-larger behemoths of the previous decade. More importantly, they could move overburden at a lower unit cost.

The 1450-W was upgraded to the 65–cubic yard (50–cubic meter) 1550-W, one of which went to England, where it became known as Big Geordie—the largest dragline in Europe at that time. The first 1570-W, with more power and range, was shipped to Drummond Coal in Alabama in 1973. This modern dragline, with booms ranging from 285 to 345 feet (87 to 105 meters) and buckets from 58 to 80 cubic yards (44 to 61 cubic meters) became a very popular mid-sized dragline, with 46 sold up to 1991.

Bucyrus-Erie introduced the first of its 1300-series walking draglines with the 1350-W in 1967. Ten of these machines, with buckets up to 60 cubic yards (46 cubic meters) and booms to 320 feet (98 meters), were shipped to locations from Texas to Suriname, from Utah to Australia. The 1350-W was upgraded to the 1370-W in 1970. Another long-running popular machine in Bucyrus' line, the 1370-W handled buckets from 58 to 65 cubic yards (44 to 50 cubic meters) on booms from 267 to 325 feet (81 to 99 cubic meters) long. Of the 38 shipped up to 1983, 23 went to Australia. In 1971, the smaller-sized 1300-W was introduced. The first of 14 of these were shipped to Peter Kiewit for coal mining in Wyoming. Two 1360-Ws with 50–cubic yard (38–cubic meter) buckets were shipped at the end of 1975, one to TransAlta's Highvale Mine in Alberta, and one to Peabody's Squaw Creek Mine in Indiana.

The massive size of the 4250-W Big Muskie can be gauged from this front view showing the operator's cab located above the two double fairleads with an entire school band positioned between the two shoes. The machine measured 151 feet from shoe to shoe, with a circular base 105 feet in diameter.

The view from inside Big
Muskie's cab could be from
any dragline. It's only when
you realize that 325 tons of
material are being dumped
from every bucketful and the
operator has the power of
24,000 horses under his
control that you appreciate
the immensity of this king of
all draglines.

The 2550-W grew into the 2560-W, and the first of two was shipped to
Peabody Coal Company in 1969. The 2560-W swung an 85–cubic yard
(65–cubic meter) bucket on a 295-foot (90-meter) boom. It worked at the
Elm Mine, Illinois, which was eventually owned by Midland Coal Company.
The model 2570-W followed, with Old Ben Coal Company in Indiana
purchasing the first. This 100–cubic yard (76–cubic meter) class 2570-W
became one of Bucyrus' most respected large machines. Twenty-seven of
these big draglines were shipped, all to customers in North America. These

included four to Consolidation Coal, Illinois, three to Associated Electric Cooperative, Missouri, and two each to Alcoa, Saskatchewan Power, Texas Utilities, North American Coal, Peabody Coal, AMAX, and Syncrude Canada.

At the top end of the scale, Bucyrus was successful in placing two huge 3270-W draglines with Amax Coal Company, who put them to work within weeks of each other in 1979. Designed on modern principles, the 3270-Ws worked at the Ayrshire Mine, Indiana, and at the Delta mine in southern Illinois. They are still the second-largest draglines in the world with their 176–cubic yard (135–cubic meter) buckets, 330-foot (101-meter) booms, and operating weight of 8,718 tons (7,909 tonnes).

MODULAR DRAGLINES

Not all dragline innovations of the past three decades were of large size. With the rapid increase in surface-mined coal in the 1970s, operators needed a machine that could quickly be dismantled and moved to a new location. Draglines taking many months to move and erect were unsuitable for small pockets of coal and short-term contracts, so the modular dragline was born. Bucyrus-Erie was first with its 380-W in 1978, followed by Marion and

This view inside Big Muskie's machinery house shows the ten hoist motors, eight drag motors and ten swing motors used to power the main digging motions. The machine utilized four drag ropes and four hoist ropes, all of 5-inch diameter. Big Muskie moved 608 million cubic yards of overburden until its retirement in 1991; this was more than double the total excavation of the Panama Canal construction.

The 1550-W of 65 cubic yards capacity was the precursor of larger draglines built to satisfy the coal boom during the Arab Oil Embargo of the early 1970s. Coal production was seen as the answer to the United States' energy crisis. One 1550-W went to England, where it was known as Big Geordie, the largest dragline in Europe at that time.

In 1973, Bucyrus upgraded the 1550-W to the 1570-W, the first of which was shipped to Drummond Coal in Alabama. The 1570-W turned out to be the most popular of Bucyrus' large walking draglines with 46 sold up to 1991. With machine upgrades over the years, bucket sizes eventually reached 80 cubic yards.

Rapier three years later. These machines all ranged in the 10– to 16–cubic yard (8– to 12–cubic meter) size and were offered with diesel or electric power. Built in modular units, the draglines were designed to be bolted instead of welded together. They could be dismantled and re-erected in a matter of a few weeks, and the diesel versions did not have to wait for a power source to be installed. These draglines fit the bill perfectly and were very popular until 1988, when the coal market softened.

Bucyrus-Erie planned to expand the modular dragline concept into larger machines. Design work was done on machines up to the 40–cubic yard (31–cubic meter) class, but the softened coal market stifled development, with only one further modular model being produced. This was the modern, computer-designed 680-W, with buckets from 20 to 25 cubic yards (15 to 19 cubic meters) depending on boom length. Five 680-Ws were sold from 1982 to 1988.

As part of its dragline redesign program to serve the coal boom in the 1970s, the 2550-W was upgraded first to the 90-yard 2560-W, and then to the 2570-W with a bucket range from 100 to 115 cubic yards. Old Ben Coal Company took delivery of the first 2570-W in 1971.

This open view of the 2570-W house shows the deck machinery arrangement. The multiple DC hoist and drag motors connect to the large bull gears of the hoist and drag drums. The vertical DC swing motors are clustered at the front, with the AC synchronous motors at the rear driving the respective DC generators.

The 2570-W circular base is typical of Bucyrus' other large draglines. The radial design of the compartments ensures minimum deflection of the circular swing rails and distributes the digging loads evenly throughout the components. This sectional view shows the placement of the swing rollers and sectional swing rack.

The 2570-W dragline utilizes the cam-and-slide propel system. An eccentric wheel rotates in a giant roller bearing to move the shoes in a circular motion. At the same time, the entire machine slides on an automatically greased path on top of the shoes, which are connected to the cam wheel by a push rod.

Bucyrus placed two of the huge 3270-W draglines in service with Amax Coal Company in 1979, one in Indiana and one in Illinois. Only slightly smaller than the record-breaking Big Muskie in terms of operating capacity, the 8,700-ton machines with 176-yard buckets are still the second largest draglines ever built.

DRAGLINE SITUATION IN THE 1980S

Recession in the 1980s caused decreased dragline sales. The world's oil crisis was over, but while coal remained the cheapest form of energy, owners experienced increasing difficulty in obtaining mine permits. The dragline market became somewhat saturated, and new machine orders dropped off dramatically. The inherent long-life of walking draglines largely contributed to this sales decrease. Those draglines placed in coal mines were of sufficient capacity to meet long-term contracts, or were designed to meet a certain constant production dictated by captive power generating stations. A dragline is designed to last about 30 years, but with major rebuilds, 50-year-old machines have been known to operate profitably. Because of their high capital cost, owners preferred to rebuild and modify components rather than buy a new machine.

Since the early 1980s, there has been a drastic shift away from coal production in the Midwest, where most of the large stripping machines operated. In order to comply with the U.S. Clean Air Act, several Midwestern power generation companies have found it cheaper to ship low-sulphur coal from the western states, particularly Wyoming, rather than convert their power stations to burn the local, high-sulphur coal. Although coal production is increasing on a yearly basis in the United States, and has done so throughout the 1990s, that increase has come from the West. Here, coal was initially

mined from thick seams under relatively shallow overburden that could be moved efficiently with trucks and shovels. As a result, with a few major exceptions, draglines have not been needed in the Western mines. This situation, however, is changing.

As mines expand into higher mining ratios (overburden moved per ton of coal mined) and some of the older mines are worked out, large walking draglines are making a comeback. A "super" version of the Bucyrus-Erie 2570-W dragline, the 2750WS, bearing little resemblance to the former model, is working at the Black Thunder Mine in Wyoming. Swinging a 160–cubic yard (122–cubic meter) bucket on a 360-foot (110-meter) boom, this dragline is the largest currently operating in North America. Several other large second-hand draglines have recently been moved to operate in the booming coal mines of Wyoming.

The coal boom of the 1970s created the need for contractors and coal companies to exploit smaller pockets of coal reserves on short-term contracts. Bucyrus responded with the modular dragline concept. The 380-W was designed with bolted modular units so it could be dismantled and moved to a new location in a matter of weeks.

Bucyrus extended the modular dragline concept to the 20- to 25-yard size when it unveiled the first 680-W in 1982. At the cutting edge of dragline technology, the 680-W featured controlled frequency AC electric power. The simple machinery layout consisted of one hoist motor, one drag motor, two swing motors and two propel motors.

In 1988, Bucyrus purchased the dragline manufacturing rights of Ransomes & Rapier Ltd. of England. This picture shows a Rapier W1800 currently working at Luscar Ltd.'s Boundary Dam Mine, Saskatchewan, Canada. When the first Rapier W1800 went to work in 1961, it was the world's largest dragline with a bucket capacity of 40 cubic yards.

RAPIER DRAGLINES PURCHASED

In 1988, Bucyrus-Erie purchased the manufacturing rights to the walking draglines designed and produced by Ransomes & Rapier Ltd. of Ipswich, England. This was an attractive buy for the company, as the Rapier-designed machines are popular in certain foreign countries, especially India, where some 15 units of the 45–cubic yard (34–cubic meter) model W2000 currently operate in coal mines.

Rapier built its first walking dragline in 1938. It featured the patented Cameron & Heath walking system, where the shoes were attached to an eccentric cam running in a roller bearing. This propel system has remained on every Rapier-designed walker to date. After introducing several other models of increasing size, Ransomes & Rapier Ltd. claimed world fame in 1951 when it announced the world's largest walking dragline, the W1400 with a 20–cubic yard (15–cubic meter) bucket on a 282-foot (86-meter) boom and an operating weight of 1,880 tons (1,706 tonnes). It was also the first dragline to be fitted with a boom made of tubular members filled with compressed gas so that, in the event of a crack occurring, the pressure loss could be relayed to the operator by a pressure gauge in his cab.

Three of the W1400 machines worked in the ironstone fields of central England. In 1961, Rapier returned with an even larger machine, the W1800, re-establishing the company as the builder of the world's largest dragline.

The current Bucyrus W2000 is a successful model carried over from the former Rapier line of walking draglines. The 45-yard machine is popular in countries such as India, where 15 currently operate in coal mines. The first W2000 was purchased in 1977 by C&K Coal Company for surface mining in Pennsylvania.

In 1940, the year after the Marion Power Shovel Company built its first walking dragline, it introduced the famous model 7400 which turned out to be one of the most successful from the company. Over 90 of the 11- to 14-yard machines were sold by 1974. In 1997, Bucyrus acquired Marion, ending a corporate rivalry that lasted 113 years.

Weighing over 2,000 tons (1,814 tonnes) and carrying a bucket of 40 cubic yards (31 cubic meters), the first W1800 went to work uncovering coal in South Wales for contractors George Wimpey & Company. Other W1800s worked on British ironstone stripping, with one still operating at Luscar Ltd.'s Boundary Dam Mine, Saskatchewan, Canada.

MARION POWER SHOVEL PURCHASED

Bucyrus' purchase of the Marion Power Shovel Company of Marion, Ohio, in 1997 drastically restructured the dragline world. This takeover, along with the earlier purchase of Rapier, meant that the number of manufacturers supplying the world's entire walking dragline needs (apart from a few in Russia) was reduced to two.

The Marion Steam Shovel Company had entered the walking dragline market in 1939 with the model 7200 swinging a 5–cubic yard (3.8–cubic meter) bucket on a 120-foot (37-meter) boom. Only three years later, Marion achieved the distinction of building the world's largest dragline up to that time, the successful model 7800, capable of swinging a 30–cubic yard (23–cubic meter) bucket on a 185-foot (56-meter) boom and weighing 1,250 tons (1,134 tonnes). The 11-cubic yard (8.4–cubic meter) 7400, launched in 1940, turned out to be one of the most popular, with more than 90 sold until 1974. In 1963, Marion startled the dragline world with

In 1963, Marion startled the world with its 85-yard capacity model 8800, a dragline substantially larger than any previously built. To move its tremendous bulk of 6,285 tons, the 8800 employed a twin shaft walking system. The machine started work at Peabody Coal's Homestead Mine in Kentucky, where it later operated with a 100-yard bucket.

The world's largest dragline currently operating is this 2570WS that was shipped to BHP Coal's Peak Downs Mine in Australia in 2000. With a maximum suspended load capability of 800,000 pounds, the dragline operates with a 160-yard bucket on a 360-foot boom. This modern-day monster boasts eight hoist, eight drag, four propel and 14 swing motors.

the model 8800. This world record beater represented a massive jump in size, with its 85–cubic yard (65–cubic meter) bucket on a 275-foot (84-meter) boom and weighing 6,285 tons (5,702 tonnes). Purchased by Peabody Coal Company for its Homestead Mine in Kentucky, it was later upgraded to a 100–cubic yard (76–cubic meter) machine. In 1965, Marion installed a 300-foot (91-meter) boom, the world's longest at that time, on a model 8700.

In 1971, Marion introduced the first of a redesigned line of 8000-series draglines featuring an eccentric cam propel system with an outboard bearing

This Bucyrus 8200 dragline receives final adjustments after erection at BNI Coal's Center Mine in North Dakota. Called Liberty, the machine filled its 77-yard bucket for the first time in November 2004. Boom length is 360 feet.

support. These included Marion's largest-ever dragline, the 150–cubic yard (115–cubic meter) 8950 with 310-foot (94-meter) boom sold to Amax Coal Company in 1973 for work at the Ayrshire Mine, Indiana. The line also included the 100–cubic yard (76–cubic meter) class 8750, first shipped in 1971 to Peabody's Universal Mine, Indiana, and the 70–cubic yard (54–cubic meter) class 8200, first shipped in 1973 to Pittsburg & Midway Coal Mining Company for work in Kansas.

The 8750 and 8200 models remained in Marion's dragline roster until the Bucyrus takeover and, along with other former Marion models, are now available as Bucyrus machines. They have received many engineering upgrades over the years, resulting in increased productivity. The modern machines carrying the same model number are hardly recognizable from their earlier counterparts. The 8750 shipped to Fording Coal's Genesee Mine, Alberta, Canada, in 1993 boasts ten swing motors mounted in the revolving frame below deck level and swings a 106–cubic yard (81–cubic meter) bucket on a boom 420 feet (128 meters) long, the longest ever installed on a dragline. The 8200, commissioned in 2004 at BNI Coal in North Dakota, digs with a 77–cubic yard (59–cubic meter) bucket suspended from a 355-foot (108-meter) boom.

In the right geological conditions, a walking dragline provides the lowest cost of stripping over-burden. The dragline remains the equipment of choice for most long-term coal stripping operations. BNI Coal's new 8200 (opposite page), and many other draglines presently operating, should still be hard at work by the time Bucyrus reaches 150 years!

CHAPTER FOUR

DRILLS

BUCYRUS ENTERS THE DRILL MARKET

Of the three major surface mining equipment lines produced today by Bucyrus, the blasthole drills are perhaps the least documented. Often, drills take second place to spectacular draglines moving millions of yards of material per year, or the huge loading shovels filling the world's largest trucks to overflow capacity in a matter of minutes. But the drills are just as important. Drills play an essential role in every hard rock mine and in most surface coal mines around the world. They work ahead of the shovel or dragline, drilling a specified pattern of holes, which are then loaded with explosives to loosen the overburden. When blasted, the material is fractured sufficiently so that it can be excavated easily by shovel or dragline. Blasting in this way is a science in itself. Large blasts must be designed to take into account the material hardness, the depth and diameter of the holes, the amount of explosive, the angle of the hole, the pattern and distance between holes, the timing delays between adjacent holes, and the safety of nearby property, personnel, and equipment.

The blasthole drills manufactured by Bucyrus have enjoyed a long and successful history. The initial product line was acquired from a company that had specialized in all types of drills and boasted a longer history than Bucyrus

Opposite: In 1933, Bucyrus-Erie acquired the Armstrong Manufacturing Company, a leading manufacturer of churn-type drills. Armstrong's predecessor companies went back to 1868, and were highly regarded in the industry. This churn-type water well drill operated by J. J. Becker was typical of the drills Bucyrus acquired.

5784-B

Since most users of shovels and draglines also needed drills, the Armstrong acquisition enabled Bucyrus-Erie to offer customers the convenience of a complete drill and excavator package from the same supplier. This busy drilling scene features a crawler-mounted Armstrong No. 29 blasthole drill, which later became the Bucyrus 29-T.

itself. This was unlike the company's other two main product lines, shovels and draglines, in which Bucyrus played a major role in developing its first machines.

Realizing the importance of drills in major excavating jobs, and the fact that most customers purchasing a shovel or dragline will also need drills, Bucyrus-Erie purchased the manufacturing rights of the Armstrong Manufacturing Company of Waterloo, Iowa, in 1933. The Armstrong company was the successor of several earlier drill manufacturers. Its heritage started in 1868 when the Kelly, Morgan & Co. of Osage, Iowa, was formed to satisfy early drilling needs of local farmers. That firm later became Morgan, Kelly and Taneyhill Co. (1891), then Armstrong Quam & Co. (1904), and finally became the Armstrong Manufacturing Company in 1910.

The acquisition provided Bucyrus-Erie with the desired blasthole drill line but also opened the door to a lucrative water well drilling market. The

line included drill tools, bit dressers, and the highly successful line of churn drills for water well and blasthole work. Armstrong was a leader in the drilling industry with many patents and innovations to its credit. It developed and patented a series of rubber-mounted shock absorbers in the derrick head to absorb the shock of the drilling tools. This was necessary when improved steel cable replaced the former manila ropes in the drill hoist. In 1922, Armstrong introduced self-propelled drilling rigs on traction wheels and, in 1927, steel-framed rigs began to replace those with wooden frames. The first Armstrong self-propelled drills with crawler tracks appeared in 1932. From 1933 to 1943, Bucyrus manufactured Armstrong drill products under the Bucyrus-Armstrong name.

This crew is shown changing drill bits of the Bucyrus-Armstrong 29-T blasthole drill on a rock excavation job. The 29-T could economically drill holes up to nine inches in diameter and became one of the most popular churn-type drills produced by the company. From its acquisition in 1933, production continued until 1959.

Bucyrus-Armstrong launched the 42-T in 1937 as a high production blasthole drill. Able to drill holes from 9 to 12 inches in diameter, its rubber shock absorbers and 48-inch stroke promised more than 50 percent increase in production over former models. Drills were sold under the Bucyrus-Armstrong name from 1933 to 1943.

DRILL LINE EXPANDS

The first Bucyrus-Armstrong drills, carried over from the former company, were known as churn-types. They included two water well drills, models 33-W and 38-W, and two blasthole drills, models 26-T and 29-T. These machines were forerunners of an expanded range of improved drills introduced by Bucyrus-Erie over subsequent years and incorporated the latest technology. The W-series models were produced for water well drilling, eventually evolving to eight different W-series machines. These small mobile drills were usually mounted on truck chassis but were also available as towed versions mounted on wheels. The most popular was the 22-W introduced in 1940. This model achieved sales of 3,492 units over a production life of 44 years.

The T-series models were churn-type blasthole drills mounted on crawler tracks. The principle of churn drill operation is quite simple. A steel rod, sharpened to a chisel point, is continuously raised and then dropped in a hole, breaking up the rock, clay, and sand particles. Water is poured into the drill hole to form a slurry from the churning action of the drill bit and the drill

This battery of 42-T blasthole drills helped A.E. Dick Construction Company move mountains of rock in the rich anthracite region of eastern Pennsylvania. The 55,000-pound 42-T was the preferred drill for rock jobs like this one, with 470 shipped until 1953. Churn-type drills were eventually replaced by modern rotary drills, which first appeared in 1952.

The oil well drilling market was another major component of Bucyrus-Armstrong's business. One of the first two oil well drills launched by the company in 1939 was the 24-L. This churn-type model could drill up to 1,500 feet and handle 1,800 pounds of tools. Most 24-Ls were either trailer- or truck-mounted, like this one owned by Anderson & Gower Inc.

cuttings. The churn drill derives its name from the up and down repetitive action of the drill stem and bit, not unlike an old-fashioned butter churn.

The 29-T, weighing 26,000 pounds (11,793 kilograms) and capable of drilling holes up to 9 inches (23 centimeters) in diameter, proved the most popular with 753 sold up to 1959. The 55,000-pound (24,948 kilogram) 42-T was introduced in 1937 and became a popular machine in rock quarries and in the hard coal areas of Pennsylvania, with 470 units sold. The big 50-T was announced in 1962 as the largest capacity mobile churn-type blasthole drill on the market. Replacing the 42-T, it could drill holes up to 12 inches (30 centimeters) in diameter and handle up to 6,000 pounds (2,722 kilograms) of tools, lifting and dropping them at a rate of 53 times per minute.

DRILL INNOVATIONS—OIL WELL DRILLS INTRODUCED

To assure straight, plumb, and parallel holes, early drills had to be hand-jacked, leveled, and supported on planks and timbers. This was time-consuming and labor intensive. Quick leveling was especially important for the blasthole drills where hole depths were relatively shallow and drill moves and setups were frequent. To ease this burden, in 1946, the 42-T became the first Bucyrus-Erie churn drill with hydraulic leveling jacks.

In 1939, Bucyrus-Erie launched its first two models of oil well drills. They were known as the 24-L and 36-L Oil Well Spudders. The 24-L could drill to 1,500-feet (457 meters) and handle 1,800 pounds (816 kilograms) of tools, while the 36-L could drill to 3,500-feet (1,067 meters) and handle 5,000 pounds (2,268 kilograms) of tools. The mobile L-series machines were often trailer-mounted and worked in conjunction with the large stationary rotary

The unique jet piercer drill was developed jointly by Bucyrus-Erie and Linde Oxygen Company in 1953. The drill was economically successful in the taconite mines of northern Minnesota and Labrador, Canada, where the short bit life of conventional drills proved unacceptable. Some 42 jet piercers were sold up to 1967, when modern rotary drills superseded the market.

The spectacular flame of the jet piercer drill is demonstrated on this model 30-J drill. The taconite is literally melted by application of an oxygen and fuel oil flame. The rock is then fractured by a localized water spray. Drilling rates of up to 20 feet per hour could be achieved, but the high cost of fuel was the machine's main disadvantage.

oil well drilling derricks, specializing in deep hole work. Initially intended for oil well purposes, the L-series drills were found equally suited for deep municipal and industrial water wells. Largest in the line was the 48-L, which could drill to 6,000 feet (1,829 meters) and handle up to 6,000 pounds (2,722 kilograms) of tools. A total of 2,984 oil well spudders were supplied by Bucyrus-Erie up to 1984 when the manufacturing rights of these models, along with the W-series water well drills, were sold to the Buckeye Drill Co. of Zanesville, Ohio.

Both the increasing number of municipal water well systems serving multiple households and the more productive rotary water well drill severely affected the churn drill industry, ending a significant era in the history of Bucyrus-Erie. But the churn drill product line had been successful beyond imagination, with 11,600 churn drills sold until 1984.

Bucyrus-Erie's best-selling drill of all time in terms of numbers sold was the 22-W water well drill. Introduced in 1940, this mobile truck-mounted rig could put down a 5-inch hole to 1,250 feet or a 12-inch hole to 400 feet. No less than 3,492 units of this model were sold until 1984.

The truck-mounted 10-R rotary-type drill was initially designed for water well drilling to 1,000 feet, but soon found a wide variety of uses. Applications included seismograph work, exploration, and oil well production. There were also special versions for blasthole and down-the-hole hammer drilling. Introduced in 1960, the 10-R stayed in production until 1981.

JET PIERCERS

While major improvements had been made in drilling productivity in most applications, extremely hard taconite ores presented special challenges. Drill penetration rates were extremely low, and bit life was unacceptable. Consequently, in 1953, Bucyrus-Erie and Linde Oxygen Co. jointly produced a jet piercer drill. A fuel oil and oxygen flame at the end of the drill pipe heated the rock, much like an acetylene torch. A localized water spray applied at the bottom of the drill hole caused the heated rock to spall and be blown out of the drill hole. This process was economically successful in drilling

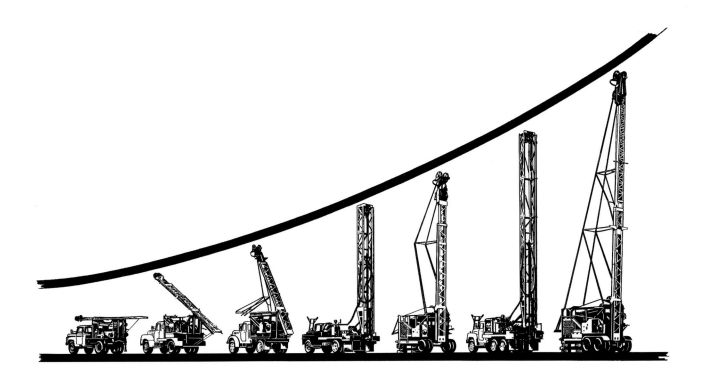

taconite, especially in the taconite mines of northern Minnesota and
Labrador, Canada, where resulting penetration rates approached 16 to 20 feet
per hour (5 to 6 meters per hour), compared with earlier churn-type drill
production of only one foot per hour (30 centimeters per hour).

Supply costs of the required fuel oil, oxygen, and water, coupled with the
often unpredictable hole diameters, limited the practical application of the jet
piercers. One hour of drill operation typically required 800 gallons (3,028 liters)
of water, 375 pounds (170 kilograms) of fuel oil, and 1250 pounds (567
kilograms) of oxygen. However, Bucyrus-Erie sold 42 jet piercers from 1954
to 1967 before the modern rotary drills with improved tungsten-carbide-insert
drill bits overtook their market.

ROTARY DRILLS INTRODUCED

Rotary drilling for oil field applications became practical with the invention
of the roller bit by Howard Hughes in 1909. Use of this technology for
blasthole applications was hampered by the need to pump wet mud through
the drill pipe and bit for the removal of the drill cuttings. The cost and time
considerations of the mud apparatus infrastructure for short depth blast holes
was usually prohibitive. The wet hole also hindered effective blasting.

The long line of Bucyrus-Erie
water well drills is depicted
in this illustration from the
heyday of their production in
the 1960s. The line included
truck- and trailer-mounted
versions and the 2400-R
and 2450-R rotary drills from
1975. In 1984, Bucyrus sold
the manufacturing rights of its
oil and water well drills to the
Buckeye Drill Company.

Bit dressing machines were an important part of any drill company's roster of equipment. Sharp tools in the hole meant maximum penetration. Two sizes of bit dressers continued from the former Armstrong line acquired in 1933. The out No. 12 could handle bits up to 12 inches in diameter and continued in production until the early 1960s.

In 1949, when the mud pump on a Joy rotary drill rig broke down, the Michigan Limestone Company conducted successful drilling experiments utilizing compressed air as the bailing agent. The 50-R, subsequently introduced by Bucyrus-Erie in 1952, was the first commercially successful large diameter, rotary blasthole drill for mining operations. It was the first in a long line of R-series blasthole drills on which today's highly-productive Bucyrus drills are founded. The giant 50-R crawler-mounted drill weighed 56 tons (51 tonnes) in operation, could put down holes up to 12 ¼ inches (31 centimeters) in diameter with bit loading to 75,000 pounds (34,019 kilograms).

As mentioned in Chapter 1, the Bucyrus-Erie 50-R attracted attention when it was used in a rescue effort in Hazelton, Pennsylvania, at the Sheppton Mine. In this emergency operation, the machine, designed to drill 12 ¼-inch (31-centimeter) holes 100 feet (30 meters) deep, produced a hole 18 inches (46 centimeters) in diameter and 330 feet (101 meters) deep. The Sheppton

rescue effort was a precursor to a similar successful mine rescue that received nationwide attention in late 2002.

In 1959, Bucyrus-Erie introduced two smaller blasthole drills similar to the 50-R. These were the 40-R in 1955 and the 30-R in 1959. All three drills employed rack and pinion hoist/pull-down systems, an obvious carryover from the crowd systems of many shovels of the day. The pull-down system allowed a heavy thrust load to be applied to the drill bit, increasing its drilling production rate. Rotational power to the rack pinions was supplied by steel cables powering a shipper shaft drum on the rotary head, again, quite similar to the shipper shaft drives on some of the earlier shovels. These drills used compressed air to blow the drilled cuttings out of the hole, so air compressors of suitable volume were installed in the machinery house.

The buoyant market of the early 1950s and the introduction of these successful rotary blasthole drills caused Bucyrus-Erie to look for additional

In 1952, Bucyrus introduced the first commercially successful large-diameter rotary blasthole drill for the mining industry. The 50-R crawler-mounted drill weighed 56 tons and was designed to put down a 12 ½-inch hole to 100 feet. Bucyrus' current blasthole drills are direct descendents of the 50-R.

Designed on similar lines to the 50-R, Bucyrus launched the smaller 40-R in 1955. The 40-R could achieve a bit loading of 50,000 pounds and handle holes from 6 ½ to 9 inches in diameter. The powerful rotary action, combined with compressed air to raise the cuttings, produced higher drilling rates than previous methods.

The 30-R blasthole drill joined its two larger brothers, the 40-R and 50-R, in 1959. All three employed a rack and pinion hoist/pull-down system, vertical hydraulic leveling cylinders, and enclosed operator's cab. Rotational drive on the 30-R was by hydraulic motor, unlike the two larger models, which were electric drive.

manufacturing space in an area with a substantial labor base. In May 1958, a brand new $12 million drill manufacturing plant was opened in Richmond, Indiana, to manufacture the entire Bucyrus-Erie drill product line. It was a superb facility, voted one of the ten best new plants in the United States for that year. But just as the plant started up, a major recession hit the drill and excavator industries, causing the market to collapse. The plant was closed the following year. Production of all the water and oil well products returned to the Evansville, Indiana, and Erie, Pennsylvania, facilities, and the rotary blasthole drill production returned to South Milwaukee, Wisconsin.

Bucyrus participated in the rotary water well drill market and produced 260 R-series type rotary water well drills, models 10-R, 2400-R, and 2450-R,

from 1960 to 1984. These models were highly mobile truck-mounted outfits with modern hydraulic controls and outriggers. The 2450-R could put down holes up to 9 inches (23 centimeters) in diameter with a pull-down capacity of 35,000 pounds (15,876 kilograms). The 10-R performed a wide variety of uses beyond water well drilling, including shallow oil production and seismograph and exploration work. It could also work with a down-the-hole hammer in tough applications.

BIG DRILLS FOR THE BOOMING COAL INDUSTRY

The need for larger drill holes spurred the introduction of the 45-R and 60-R drill models in the 1960s. The larger, more efficiently produced blast holes, combined with more effective blasting agents, resulted in greater blasting productivity. The 60-R and its dual motor rotary drive and dual air compressor brother, the 61-R, became workhorses of the surface mining industry.

The big 61-R appeared in 1962 and was capable of 90,000 pounds of bit loading and drilling holes up to 15 inches in diameter. Shipped until 1987, upgrades through Series IV machines increased bit loading to 130,000 pounds for holes up to 17 ½ inches. The 61-R boasted dual air compressors and dual-motor rotary drive.

The 60-R was similar to the 61-R except it ran with a single air compressor and single-motor rotary drive for economy in operation. It could achieve maximum bit loading of 125,000 pounds and produce drill holes up to 15 inches in diameter. Production years spanned from 1962 to 1993, with upgrades to the Series IV machines.

Between 1962 and 1993, 374 of the 60-R/61-R drills were produced. They could drill holes to 17 ½ inches (44 centimeters) in diameter with bit loading to 130,000 pounds (58,967 kilograms). The majority of big blasthole drills were powered by electricity. The trail cable could be stored conveniently on the optional cable reel at the front of the machine. Electric motors on the machine rotated the drill pipe and bit, while another motor propelled the machine, as well as raised or lowered the drill bit out of the drill hole. A third motor powered the air compressor for bailing the hole (blowing out the rock chips).

The advanced 49-HR is a heavy-duty blasthole drill designed for 60-foot single pass drilling of 16-inch diameter hole. It features a chainless pull-down system and programmable logic control which manages and monitors all drill functions and performs diagnostic reporting. The 49-R series appeared in 1986 with bit loading capability to 120,000 pounds.

Announced in 1996, the 39 series drill is a highly mobile, diesel-hydraulic blasthole drill designed for medium-sized holes up to 12 ¼ inches in diameter and offering bit loading to 90,000 pounds. Its most distinguishing feature is a new mast design with tubular members arranged in a triangular structure similar to Bucyrus' patented dragline boom design.

Two massive 67-R's were shipped to an Australian coal mine in the mid 1980s. They were the largest drills ever made by Bucyrus, but only these two were produced. Based on the time-proven 60-R, the 67-R was the super drill of the 1980s. Its high productivity, with bit loading to 160,000 pounds (72,575 kilograms) and a 17 ½-inch (44-centimeter) hole capability, was matched with operator comforts, including a hot plate, refrigerator, microwave, and wash basin.

Contrary to the water well drill market trend, the blasthole drill market remained strong. A new generation model 49-R drill was introduced in 1986 and incorporated radical design changes. Its features and design philosophies evolved from the results of an in-depth marketing study encompassing over 70 different mining companies. Bucyrus-Erie commissioned an industrial design firm to enhance the new image with a fresh outward appearance. The final result was an efficient, reliable, and productive machine, poised for the future growth of the industry. The current 49-HR has a bit loading capacity of 141,000 pounds (63,957 kilograms).

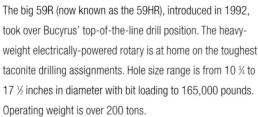

The big 59R (now known as the 59HR), introduced in 1992, took over Bucyrus' top-of-the-line drill position. The heavy-weight electrically-powered rotary is at home on the toughest taconite drilling assignments. Hole size range is from 10 ¾ to 17 ½ inches in diameter with bit loading to 165,000 pounds. Operating weight is over 200 tons.

Newest in Bucyrus' drill line is the unique diesel-powered 39HR with a triangular mast. With all functions powered hydraulically, the 39HR can perform single pass drilling of up to 35 feet for holes from 9 to 13 ¾ inches in diameter. With a working weight of 150 tons, the 39HR can impart a bit loading of 122,000 pounds.

MODERN DRILLS

In 2003, Bucyrus produced its 100th 49-R drill. This model continues to be the mainstay of high-production blasthole drilling at mines around the world. It was joined in 1992 by the 59-R, currently Bucyrus' flagship drill. This massive 59-R weighs up to 200 tons (181 tonnes), and produces 17 ½-inch (44-centimeter) holes with a bit loading of 165,000 pounds (74,843 kilograms). Its main use has been in taconite mines.

Bucyrus' drill history has been rich, varied, and successful. Bucyrus drill products have been shipped worldwide to every country in which mining plays a significant role. Designing and building the most productive, efficient, reliable, and cost-effective blasthole drills in the industry remains a continuing challenge and company focus.

The 49HR is the latest version of the successful electrically-powered 49-R rotary blasthole drills. It maintains all the features of the former model, such as hydraulic propel and automatic leveling, but boasts increased specifications such as bit loading to 141,000 pounds, and single pass drilling to 65 feet deep. The one shown is working for Titania in Norway.

POSTSCRIPT
THE FUTURE

For 125 years, Bucyrus has been a world leader in bringing new technology to the surface mining industry. Bucyrus-designed and -built machines reduce support and maintenance costs while improving productivity and the customer's bottom line. Current research and development efforts are laying the foundation for Bucyrus to provide the industry with the lowest cost-per-ton of material moved for another 125 years.

An excellent example of this long-range development is the 495 High-Performance shovel, created from a combination of the 395B/495B-series upper works and the original Marion 301M/351M lower works (which was at the forefront of technology when launched in 1986). The 495's updated technology includes planetary gear configurations, IGBT electrics, AccessDirect (the latest in maintenance support technology), and an optional hydraulic crowd system to enhance shovel operation through increased efficiency and lower maintenance costs. Several available configurations allow the 495 series be customized to each customer's unique application.

As the final pages were being completed for this book, Bucyrus announced a major expansion program at the South Milwaukee, Wisconsin, facility. In a phased expansion program Bucyrus plans to create a plant to be known as the Rawson Avenue facility to initially include 110,000 square feet of new manufacturing and welding space. When the phased expansion is completed, the new facility and grounds will encompass a total 351,000 square feet of manufacturing welding and storage space.

Bucyrus also brings the latest dragline technology to market. With the former Marion and Rapier designs under its wing, Bucyrus is able to offer machines with the best features from each design. A new 8750D being shipped to China at the time of this writing is a perfect example. This dragline carries a 117–cubic yard (89–cubic meter) bucket and is the first large dragline to be entirely powered with a Siemens AC static drive system. It introduces the first gearless direct drive for draglines, the D^3 system, for the hoist and drag motions, using the latest technology to substantially increase productivity while reducing support costs.

The Bucyrus drill line sets the industry benchmark for large rotary blasthole drills. The 39HR drill is designed for flexibility and maneuverability. Its mast, unique in the industry, was made possible by combining drill design with existing dragline boom technology. The mast is built of tubular members arranged in a triangular fashion to form an inherently sound structure—just as booms have been built for decades—enabling it to withstand torsional, compressive, tensile, and bending stresses. Field reports have been very positive. A recent 39HR update has simplified hydraulics and piping, resulting in increased reliability, positioning this drill for future long-term reliability.

Looking far into the future requires a vivid imagination. With 125 years of experience and dedication, Bucyrus has harnessed that imagination. Advanced computer technology will continue to enhance production reporting, diagnostic reporting, and increased automation. These advances will bring greater operator comfort, increased safety, and decreasing levels of pollution. As long as there is a need to move earth to extract minerals, Bucyrus will design and deliver the machines needed by the surface mining industry.

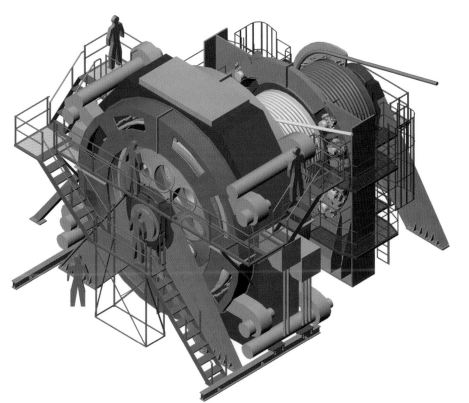

The first gearless drive for walking dragline hoist and drag drums is being installed on a machine to be commissioned in 2006. The AC system controls high-torque motors through Siemens AC electrical technology, resulting in faster cycle times. With maintenance costs reduced by eliminating hoist and drag gearing, this next generation in dragline technology promises new levels of productivity.

APPENDIX A

FIRST & CURRENT BOARDS OF DIRECTORS

Seated (left to right): Tim Sullivan, Ted Rogers, Robert Purdum
Standing (left to right): Gene Little, Ronald Crutcher, Edward Nelson, Robert Korthals
Not pictured: Robert Scharp

2005 BOARD OF DIRECTORS

THEODORE C. ROGERS is Chairman and Director of American Industrial Partners and has been a Director of Bucyrus since 1997. Mr. Rogers has served as Chairman of the Board since 2004.

TIMOTHY W. SULLIVAN is President and Chief Executive Officer of Bucyrus International, Inc. and has been a Director of Bucyrus since 2000.

RONALD A. CRUTCHER is the President of Wheaton College, a private, national liberal arts college in Norton, Massachusetts, and has been a Director of Bucyrus since 2004.

ROBERT W. KORTHALS is the non-executive Chairman of the Ontario Teachers' Pension Plan Board and has been a Director of Bucyrus since 2004.

GENE E. LITTLE is a Director and Audit Committee member of Great Lakes Carbon Corporation, a producer of calcined petroleum coke for use in aluminum smelting; Director and member of the Audit Committee of Unizan Financial Corp., a financial services holding company; and has been a Director of Bucyrus since 2004.

EDWARD G. NELSON is President and Chairman of the Board of Nelson Capital Corp., a merchant banking firm, and has been a Director of Bucyrus since 2004.

ROBERT L. PURDUM is a Managing Director of American Industrial Partners and has been a Director of Bucyrus since 1997.

ROBERT C. SCHARP currently serves as Chairman of Shell Canada's Mining Advisory Council and was recently appointed as a Director of Bucyrus in 2005.

2005 EXECUTIVE MANAGEMENT

Timothy W. Sullivan—President and Chief Executive Officer

Thomas B. Phillips—Executive Vice President and Chief Operating Officer

Craig Mackus—Chief Financial Officer, Controller, and Secretary

Frank P. Bruno—Vice President Human Resources

John F. Bosbous—Treasurer

1880 BOARD OF DIRECTORS

W. H. Harris

J. B. Gormly

H. P. Eells

A. St. J. Newbury

D. P. Eells (primary Founder of Bucyrus Foundry and Manufacturing Co.)

S. W. Crittenden

W. B. Crittenden

J. Thompson

D. P. Eells

1880 EXECUTIVE MANAGEMENT

W. H. Harris—President 1880–1895

W. B. Crittenden—Secretary 1880–1893 and Treasurer 1880–1888

D. P. Eells—Vice President 1883–1888 (served in various additional capacities until 1952)

H. P. Eells—Vice President 1888–1896 and Treasurer 1888–1896 (served in various additional capacities until 1919)

APPENDIX B

A TRIBUTE TO WILLIAM WHEELER COLEMAN (1873–1964)

Bucyrus has been led by many talented managers and directors over the years, but W. W. Coleman stands out as a primary contributor to the success and longevity of what has become Bucyrus International Inc.

Mr. Coleman served the company for sixty years, forty-six of those as the president and chairman of the board. Prior to joining Bucyrus, he worked as an engineer and metallurgist, ; and consequently, he started his tenure with Bucyrus as foundry superintendent in 1905. He was promoted to works manager in 1907 and to second vice president in 1909. During 1910 he gained experience in sales promotion, engineering, manufacturing, and purchasing, and by 1911 he became president at the age of 38. His last year as chairman was 1957, after which he served as a member of the executive committee. In 1962, Coleman became honorary life chairman; he passed away in December 1964.

Bucyrus achieved its world leadership in the industry primarily as a result of Coleman's foresight and business acumen. It was Coleman who, in 1911, assumed responsibility for consolidating the newly-merged Vulcan and Atlantic companies into an effective organization. In 1922, he overruled the decision of his board of directors to close the Evansville plant after several loss-making years; he instead initiated measures to raise the plant's efficiency and modernize its product line. Within a short time the plant returned to profitability and became an essential manufacturing base for the following six decades. Coleman also initiated strategic acquisitions such as Erie Steam Shovel Company, Monighan Manufacturing Company, and Armstrong Drill Company, whose products not only complimented Bucyrus' existing line but became the backbone of today's dragline and drill products. Coleman recognized the importance of a strong presence in the United Kingdom and opened a London office in 1919, greatly enhancing export sales. He later spearheaded the merger with Ruston & Hornsby and established Ruston-Bucyrus Ltd. in Lincoln, England.

Throughout his years as chairman and president, Coleman never lost sight of the mandate on which the company was founded: to focus on the manufacture of machines that move the earth. He guided the company, sometimes single-handedly, through periods of depression and prosperity in an industry notorious for its cyclical business climate. Coleman developed a corporate culture and business strategy that has enabled Bucyrus to not only survive well beyond most of its competitors, but also prosper as the dynamic entity known today as Bucyrus International Inc. William Wheeler Coleman, one of America's great industrial leaders, was a true "Bucyrus Warrior."

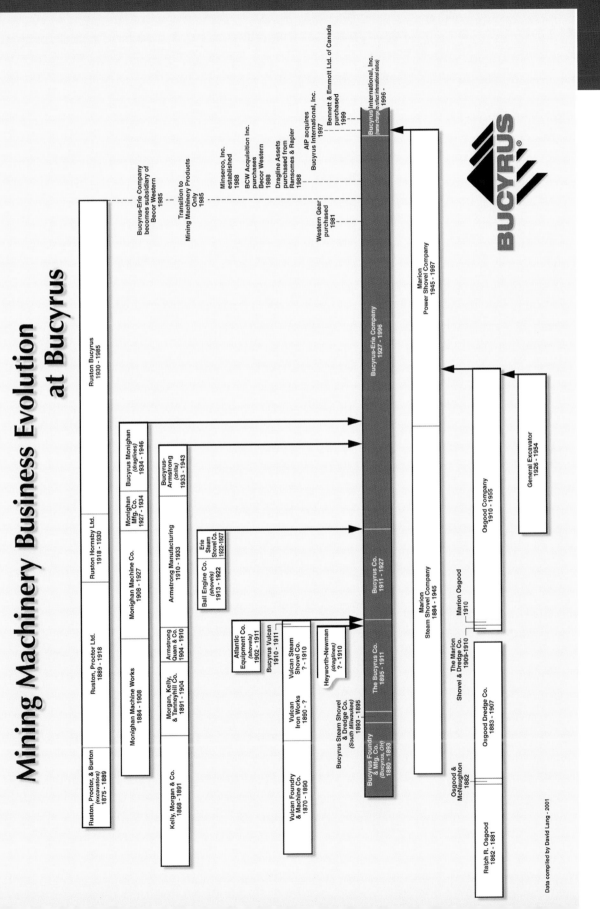

Mining Machinery Business Evolution at Bucyrus

Data compiled by David Lang - 2001

MINING SHOVEL, WALKING DRAGLINE, & DRILL MODELS (PAST & PRESENT)

MINING SHOVELS

BUCYRUS & BUCYRUS-ERIE ELECTRIC MINING & STRIPPING SHOVELS

DIPPER MODEL	RANGE* CUBIC YARDS	FIRST SHIPPED	LAST SHIPPED	NOTES
50-B	1 3/4	1922	1934	Steam, gas, diesel or electric power
75-B	2 1/4	1928	1935	
80-B	2–2 1/2	1921	1929	Steam or electric power
85-B	3 1/4	1935	1957	
100-B	3 1/2–4	1926	1950	Steam or electric power
110-B	4–7	1950	1975	
120-B	5–8	1925	1951	Steam or electric power
150-B (Old)	2 1/2	1911	1924	Stripping shovel. Steam powered
150-B	6–10	1951	1975	
155-B	9–15	1975	1982	
170-B	6 1/2–10	1929	1951	
175-B	3 1/2	1912	1925	Stripping shovel. Steam or electric power
182M	10–23	1996	Current	Former Marion 182-M introduced 1966
190-B	9–15	1952	1976	
195-B/B1	13–26	1968	1998	
200-B (Old)	7	1927	1943	Stripping shovel
225-B	6	1914	1923	Stripping shovel. Steam or electric power
270-B	8–18	1960	1962	
280-B	8–18	1962	1982	
290-B/B1/B2	10–20	1976	1983	
295-B/B1/B2	16–51	1972	Current	
320-B	8	1923	1930	Stripping shovel. Steam or electric power
375-B	7	1929	1940	Stripping shovel
385-B	12	1929	1929	Stripping shovel. One built.
395-B/B1/B2/B3	34–44	1979	1998	
495-B/B1/B2	25–80	1990	2002	
495HD/HR/HF	40–80	2002	Current	Rating: HD 90 tons, HR & HF 110–120 tons
550-B	11–27	1936	1954	Stripping shovel.
595-B	60	1997	2001	Former Marion 351M/301M introduced 1986
750-B I	12–16	1927	1930	Stripping shovel. Non-counterbalanced hoist
750-B II	18–20	1930	1940	Stripping shovel. Counterbalanced hoist
950-B	30–36	1935	1941	Stripping shovel. Counterbalanced hoist
1050-B	26–45	1941	1960	Stripping shovel. Counterbalanced hoist
1650-B	55–70	1956	1964	Stripping shovel.
1850-B	90	1963	1963	Stripping shovel. One built.
1950-B	105	1965	1965	Stripping shovel. One built.
1950-B	130	1967	1967	Stripping shovel. One built.
3850-B	115	1962	1962	Stripping shovel. One built.
3850-B	140	1964	1964	Stripping shovel. One built.

Note: Dipper capacities vary with material density and boom length.

BUCKET MODEL	RANGE* CUBIC YARDS	FIRST SHIPPED	LAST SHIPPED	NOTES
1-T	1	1913	1925	
1 1/2 -T	1 1/2–2	1922	1924	
2-T	2	1915	1922	
2 1/2 T	2 1/2	1922	1922	
3-T	3	1913	1925	
3 1/2 T	3 1/2	1922	1922	
4-T	4	1924	1925	
1-W	1	1926	1926	
1 1/2 -W	1 1/2	1926	1926	
2-W	2–2 1/2	1926	1938	
3-W	3–3 1/2	1925	1944	
4-W	4	1926	1932	
5-W	4–6	1934	1948	
6-W	5–6	1926	1934	
7-W	6–7	1942	1971	
9-W	8–10	1938	1954	
10-W	8–12	1934	1939	
15-W	12–14	1940	1940	
6150	6–8	1929	1932	
6160	6–8	1932	1938	
8160	8–10	1931	1931	
180-W	4 1/2–6	1954	1965	
200-W	4 1/2–6	1945	1956	
380-W	10–16	1978	1985	
450-W	9–12	1948	1954	
480-W	13–18	1955	1979	
500-W	12–14	1946	1959	
650-B	15–17	1946	1954	
680-W	34–40	1982	Current	
770-B	19–21	1954	1965	
800-W	28	1966	1970	
950-B	12	1935	1935	
1150-B	20–25	1944	1950	
1250-B	25–38	1951	1958	
1250-W	35	1959	1963	
1260-W	30–40	1965	1990	
1300-W	33–47	1971	1985	
1350-W	45–60	1967	1977	
1360-W	50	1975	1976	
1370-W	58–65	1970	1984	
1450-W	60	1963	1968	
1500-W	70	1970	1971	
1550-W	65	1968	1968	
1570-W	58–80	1973	1991	
2550-W	75	1964	1966	
2560-W	85–90	1969	1969	
2570-W	100–115	1971	1983	
2570WS	140–160	1990	Current	
3270-W	176	1977	1977	
4250-W	220	1968	1968	
W2000	31–44	1988	Current	Former Rapier W2000 introduced 1977
7820	32–44	1997	Current	Former Marion 7820 introduced 1970
8050	51–64	1997	Current	Former Marion 8050 introduced 1970
8200	65–94	1997	Current	Former Marion 8200 introduced 1973
8400	60–80	1969	1971	
8750/8750D	80–135	1997	Current	Former Marion 8750 introduced 1971
8750H/8750HD	140	2005	Current	"D" models have AC direct drum drive.

* Bucket size depends on material density and working radius.

FIRST MODEL	LAST SHIPPED	SHIPPED	NOTES
1-W	1955	1961	Water well drill
20-W	1949	1981	Water well drill
21-W	1935	1949	Water well drill
22-W	1940	1984	Water well drill
24-W	1938	1943	Water well drill
29-W	1935	1941	Water well drill
33-W	1933	1939	Water well drill
38-W	1933	1941	Water well drill
10-R	1960	1981	Water well drill
10-RH	1960	1981	Water well drill
2400-R	1975	1984	Water well drill
2450-R	1975	1984	Water well drill
24-L	1939	1953	Oil well drill
28-L	1945	1971	Oil well drill
36-L	1939	1984	Oil well drill
60-L	1953	1972	Oil well drill
48-L	1945	1959	Oil well drill
JPM-3	1953	1960	Jet Piercer
JPM-4	1962	1967	Jet Piercer
23-P	1937	1941	Prospecting drill
26-P	1937	1937	Prospecting drill
27-P	1939	1939	Prospecting drill
22-T	1942	1962	Blast hole drill, churn type
26-T	1933	1937	Blast hole drill, churn type
27-T	1937	1961	Blast hole drill, churn type
29-T	1933	1959	Blast hole drill, churn type
42-T	1937	1953	Blast hole drill, churn type
50-T	1953	1964	Blast hole drill, churn type
30-R	1959	1974	Blast hole drill, rotary type
35-R	1986	2003	Blast hole drill, rotary type
35HR	2004	Current	Blast hole drill, rotary type
39-R	1996	2003	Blast hole drill, rotary type
39HR	2004	Current	Blast hole drill, rotary type
40-R	1955	1984	Blast hole drill, rotary type
45-R	1966	1989	Blast hole drill, rotary type
47-R	1983	1991	Blast hole drill, rotary type
49-R/HR	1986	Current	Blast hole drill, rotary type
50-R	1952	1972	Blast hole drill, rotary type
55-R	1972	1985	Blast hole drill, rotary type
59-R/HR	1992	Current	Blast hole drill, rotary type
60-R	1962	1993	Blast hole drill, rotary type
61-R	1962	1987	Blast hole drill, rotary type
67-R	1986	1987	Blast hole drill, rotary type

GENERAL INDEX